First Light

Prayers from
New Christian Communities

edited by
ELDRED WILLEY

DARTON·LONGMAN + TODD

First published in 2001 by
Darton, Longman and Todd Ltd
1 Spencer Court
140–142 Wandsworth High Street
London SW18 4JJ

ISBN 0–232–52412–2

A catalogue record for this book is available from the British Library.

Illustrated by Leigh Hurlock
Designed by Sandie Boccacci
Phototypeset in 10/13pt Myriad Light by Intype London Ltd
Printed and bound in Great Britain by
The Cromwell Press, Trowbridge, Wiltshire

Contents

Foreword

Here is a book to enrich you, a book about living in community and in relationship with God. Come and meet some of the people who are seeking to maintain community and a depth of meaning in our fragmented society. Come and share in their search and in their prayers: you will be able to discover what they count as their riches and how they seek to communicate this treasure to the large community around them. Above all, you will be invited to come with them before God, for all of them have a deep prayer life and a desire to praise and proclaim Father, Son and Holy Spirit. They are not people running away from the world, they are seeking to enter deeper into the world and its true meaning. Whilst most of humankind is skating on the surface of life, here are groups of people who seek to plumb its depths. Let them help you to come to deeper reality. Whilst so many are playing with virtual reality here are communities seeking the reality itself and discovering that such a search leads them to God.

First Light is full of the riches of new Christian communities and the freshness of faith they have to offer. Throughout these pages, you will be given the opportunity to travel with the communities through the Christian year, to face momentous occasions and special days. More than this, you will share in their innermost hopes and desires and see them seeking to reach out to a lonely society, where community is endangered or breaking down. This is a book about communication and fellowship and a book of mission. Here are various groups of people who have learnt of the love of God and cannot keep it to themselves.

Modern society lives closer together and has more means of immediate communication than any age before it, yet communication and community life are both endangered. It is good to discover a book that looks at the upsurge in new communities and what they have to say to any who would stop and listen. Here is a chance to meet some well-established communities, some of them new that may only be here for a while, and to discover that all have something to offer. There is a list of addresses at the back of the book so that you can actually visit or contact a community that interests you. You can move from a Roman Catholic to an Orthodox community and on to a Church of Scotland, Anglican or Methodist community. Others are definitely ecumenical and many of them are probing the borders of reality.

This is a book for all who are involved in the building up of community and for all who are travelling through the Christian calendar and seeking to make it relevant to the people around them. There is no doubt that time with this book will enrich your thinking and your worship.

DAVID ADAM
Holy Island

Introduction

Life is very short. So if we want to do something with God, we had best do it now.

It is out of such a conviction that Christian communities are born. In the past they have frequently been started by an individual – or a married couple – going all out for God, and drawing together a few followers. The little group tends its hearth for a few years until sheer human frailty leaves it empty.

Today we still see some of these transient communities, but we also see something new. Several of the movements represented here have let their seeds carry on the wind, and are now rooted in scores of countries. What they will grow into is anybody's guess: nothing quite like this has happened before.

In this book we also come across new religious orders, two of which – the Sisters of the Gospel of Life and the Franciscan Friars of the Renewal – sprang up in Britain during the Jubilee Year 2000. They have appeared to meet the new challenges of our time – the loss of the sense of the sacred and the threat to unborn life – and also, as the Franciscans express it, to challenge the worldly values which are prevalent in every age.

Of the communities in this collection, one of the first to be founded was Iona. Like others which have endured – Hengrave, Cornerstone, Maranatha – it carries in its heart a deep longing for reconciliation between divided Christians. Perhaps what we most need now are generous gestures from all sides which express that longing. Maybe, too, we have to put a time limit on unforgiveness. Copyright expires 70 years after the death of the author, but communal grudges between Christians, it seems, remain valid for ever.

Some of the prayers in this book will startle, like a simple sari in an Oxford Street boutique. That is because holiness is out of fashion. Indeed, reading many spiritual writers today, you would imagine it is something which educated people grow out of. Here, then, is an alternative perspective.

Any Christian picking up this book cannot fail to be tremendously encouraged. For, whatever the press may print, here is evidence that God has not finished with these islands. Above all, however, these prayers are a celebration of God's goodness. They are a reminder that he does not leave us in our isolation and despair, but comes to be with us. And he gives us each other. He sets the lonely in families.

And these families – where hearts have grown cold – keep alive the unheard-of, unimaginable possibility that love exists.

Using this book

Those who are familiar with the Prayer of the Church will quickly find their way around this book, since it follows the same pattern. For those who are not, it may serve as an introduction to a daily and seasonal rhythm of prayer. Its incompleteness is fortunate, for it is not meant to be an alternative to any official daily prayer book. The purpose is simply to enrich.

A healthy Christian community is a place of creativity. Those who have fashioned unique ways of living and working together will also fashion unique ways of worshipping together. And so this book has some additional sections.

One gathers together community prayers – those which encapsulate the identities of the particular communities. A second is for young people, who will always have a culture which stands slightly apart.

The primary vocation of the communities represented here – as the Sisters of the Gospel of Life express it so well – is to centre their lives on Jesus Christ. They are not pressure groups. But the very fact that they are rooted in Christ means that they are the more rooted in the reality of the world and its pain. Hence a third section, 'We care passionately about...'. In the concerns expressed here – for evangelisation, the family and the poor, for example – we may hear something of what the Spirit is saying to the Churches.

In the past, God spoke in fragmentary and varied fashion through the prophets, and he does so in a similar way, I believe, through this book. If we only hear in snatches, no matter. For now he has also spoken to us through his Son. My hope is that this collection will be a pointer towards him.

Seasons

Advent

Open our eyes

Open our eyes, Lord,
especially if they are half-shut
      because we are tired of looking,
or half-open
      because we fear to see too much,
or bleared with tears
      because yesterday and today and tomorrow
      are filled with the same pain,
or contracted,
      because we only look at what we want to see.

Open our eyes, Lord,
to gently scan the life we lead,
      the home we have,
      the world we inhabit,
and so to find,
among the gremlins and the greyness,
signs of hope we can fasten on and encourage.

Give us, whose eyes are dimmed by familiarity,
a bigger vision of what you can do,
even with hopeless cases and lost causes
and people of limited ability.

Pause.

Show us the world as in your sight,
riddled by debt, doubt and disbelief,
yet also
shot through with possibility
for recovery, renewal, redemption.

Pause.

And lest we fail to distinguish vision from fantasy,

today, tomorrow, this week,
    open our eyes to one person,
    or one place,
where we – being even for a moment prophetic –
might identify and wean a potential in the waiting.

Pause.

And with all this,
open our eyes, in yearning, for Jesus.

Pause.

On the mountains,
in the cities,
through the corridors of power
and streets of despair,
to help, to heal,
to confront, to convert,
O come, O come Immanuel.

From the Iona Community

New beginnings

Father,
protect your Church,
so that we may have a clear spirit
and again and again find
forgiveness of sins and
a new beginning
through
your great grace.
Give us a clear conscience
and always
a clear new beginning in you.
For we honour and praise you
and want to be yours.
To you be glory and honour and praise.
Amen.

From the Darvell Bruderhof

The light of Christ

If you can see the difference
Between darkness and light;
If you can feel the difference
Between a hand that strikes
And a hand that strokes,
Then, whatever your condition,
You can begin to know God.
I saw a puddle of mud
Sun-struck and bright as the Star of Bethlehem,
And I thought, even so,
The light of Christ has come into the world,
And wherever a man breathes,
And a woman feels,
There is hope.

For those who have not heard the good news,
The hostile and unforgiving,
The cold, lethargic, apathetic,
The desperately unhappy,
The evil, the mad
And all who are out of kilter with society,
For all these, and for us all
He died
And lives still.
Nothing, no one is hopeless,
All may be redeemed from their darkness
By his light.
From the Hengrave Community

Star kindler

O God, star kindler
kindle a flame of love within us
to light our path in days of darkness.

O God, sun warmer
warm us with your love
to melt the frozen hand of guilt.

O God, moon burnisher
burnish the shield of faith
that we may seek justice
and follow the ways of peace.
From the Iona Community

Christmas

Child of hope

Welcome, child of hope,
Born in this dark and dreary month,
Conceived at a time
When hope was wearing thin.
The hope of your coming
Has sustained a weary nation
Through a long, dark winter.

And now you come,
Bringing joy to a nation
Which has known so much sorrow:
You make our barren, weary hearts
Sing anew with joy.
Tiny, insignificant,
Known to a select few,
You turn lives upside-down.
Welcome, child of hope.
From the Hengrave Community

So Joseph cradled Mary

In the bleak midwinter
Their journey felt too long;
So Joseph cradled Mary
With love and murmured song;
As Mary's womb gave Jesus,
May we now birth the word;
A power which has transfigured all
Who to its light deferred.

The travellers, hid outwith the walls,
Are led there with their flock;
The fourth world of the people
Realise he's Jesse's stock;

Whose parents share their standing
As refugees reviled,
Turfed out by force of circumstance,
A homeless couple with their child.

The kings must come a long way,
As rich folk often do,
To give up plans and privilege
And dream of journeys new;
The gift for our thanksgiving –
Community restored;
The Spirit gives us freedom to
Remember or betray our Lord.

From L'Arche Edinburgh

Echo of the angels' song

May these days of Christmas,
days which remind us of Jesus' first appearance on earth,
be more than ever
days of profound inner and outer joy,
an echo of the angels' song and of the shepherds' gladness!

May we live them so that Jesus,
now ascended into heaven,
when he looks down on earth
and on all the places celebrating this Christmas,
will rest his gaze with particular satisfaction
on the place where we are staying,
so he can admire
a marvellous, living Christmas,
built and re-built, hour by hour,
out of our love for one another,
which makes him really present among us.

From the Focolare Movement

Caravans of wealth

This may be sung to the tune 'Quem Pastores'.

Caravans of wealth appearing;
Shepherds from a lowland shieling;

Shoot of royal stock is brearing;
Sign revealed by silver light.

Skirting towns and travelling onwards,
Searching for a God among us;
No one knew his name was Jesus –
God with us in human need.

Only God would christen Jesus
With a name that faith reveals as
Saviour of all pilgrim people:
Those who trek by silver light.

Heartbeat close his parents cradle
Jesus, born within a stable;
See the cult of power disabled –
God is born for human kind.

Stars appear and promise daybreak,
Violent soldiers herald heartache;
Cries of anguish pierce the darkness;
Where is God in human need?

Word made flesh, our gifts revealing,
Mary, Joseph, persevering,
All who find God's gift amazing
Turn for home by unknown ways.

From L'Arche Edinburgh

New Year

Prayer for the last day of the year

Another year goes into the chasm of eternity. What have I done with it, my Lord and my God? Today you gave me a glimpse of my nothingness, my utter inadequacy, my hopelessness in your service.

How can you, my Lord, have patience with such as I? I know your patience and mercy are infinite. But look at my vanity, self-love, indulgences of all kinds. Look at the graces you have showered on me, and look at the lack of co-operation on my part.

Look at my unworthiness; look at your kindness, Jesus, Son of man, my Lord and my God. Forgive me and accept my thanks for allowing me another chance, another year. I know my weakness. I know that without you I am nothing. Help me. Alone I cannot make one step. Let me see myself as I am.

Make me realise these graces that you have allowed. Give me tolerance, understanding, humility, patience. Above all, inflame my heart with an unquenchable love for you. Make me an alert servant, not a sloppy, tired, lazy one as I have been until now. Do not allow me, sweet Lord, to take unto myself any pride about my achievement. Make me humbly realise that I am only an instrument. You know it is all for your glory.

Make me more charitable, more gentle, more understanding with people. Give me humility – then I shall be able to serve you as I should. Cure my laziness. Give me strength and determination for sacrifices and mortifications. Make me patient, controlling all irritability, anger, impatience.

Help me, O master. Look not at the unworthiness of your servant but only on my desire to serve you. Enkindle that desire until, as a flame, it consumes me entirely. Bless all the things I do in your name. Give me understanding of what I should do and what I should run away from. Give me your love. In temporal things, give me my daily bread, and rest as you will. Your will be done, not mine.

From the Madonna House Community

Prayer for the New Year

Dear Jesus, I have done so little for you in the past year. I do not know what you have in store for me in this coming year, yet I accept beforehand its joys, sacrifices, sorrows, pains – and even death, if it is your will.

You will help me to do my part and co-operate with your grace, refrain from my habitual sins, overcome my faults and defects. O Jesus, you know that without you I am nothing. Be with me. Allow me to spend this coming year in your love and service, without counting the cost.

Bless me and my family, and those with whom I will come in contact – especially those who may dislike me. They have good reasons! Bring to your feet those who seek you, groping for your love and light.

Bless and help the dying, the poor, the sick I will meet. Give the gift of holiness to all the priests I know. Bless all those who love me and help me. Give strength, health and wisdom to the Pope and bishops. Bless this house and all who live here. Let me always remember that all I am, all that I have, are yours.

From the Madonna House Community

Lent

Prepare us for your way

The words in bold may be said all together.

Lord, you know that we love you
and we know what you ask us to do …
But for those times when we have been too busy
when we have been too hard-hearted
when we have been lukewarm
we say sorry
and ask for your forgiving love.
Prepare us for your way, O Lord.
>   **Your kingdom come, your will be done.**

Lord, you know our good intentions
and we know your will …
But hold us back long enough to listen to those in need
and to learn from them
and to learn of our own need.
Where we think we are sent, make us ready to receive,
where we are keen to teach, make us ready to learn.
Prepare us for your way, O Lord.
>   **Your kingdom come, your will be done.**

Lord, you know our deepest desires
and we know the vision of your kingdom …
We bring before you those elements in our lives
in need of your transforming power:
that which we misuse or neglect,
that which we most reluctantly let go of,
that which we believe is not good enough:
inspire us and disturb us to examine our deepest desires.
Prepare us for your way, O Lord.
>   **Your kingdom come, your will be done.**

Lord, you know our potential
but what is your purpose for our lives?

In our uncertainty
and in the knowledge of your faithfulness
prepare us for your way, O Lord.
     Your kingdom come, your will be done.

From the Iona Community

The graces of Lent

Beloved, today I want to thank you for the great graces of Lent. This Lent has been so precious to me, so wonderful. Hidden truths have become clear, and my own heart's desire clarified: you!

O Beloved, thank you for your kindness, your mercy, your forgiveness, your love. I ask of you only one gift for myself as we approach Easter: to love you ever more! I offer you the poorest gift anyone ever gave – my heart.

You asked for it when you said, 'I am thirsty.' It is yours to do with as you wish. Only, with the penitent thief, I repeat, 'Lord, remember me when you come into your kingdom.'

I love, love, love you, and I rejoice today at the approaching beauty of your resurrection.

From the Madonna House Community

We have to change

Our Father in heaven,
We thank you for your Gospel
That tells us we have to change.
Each one personally has to change
So that we may all come
Under your government
And under your leadership.
Father, grant that Jesus,
With his eyes of fire,
May look deep into our hearts
To see everything that is there
And to change everything,
Even if we have to go
Through judgement.
Make us yours.

May we always belong to you.
Amen.

From the Darvell Bruderhof

I have found you

I have found you in so many places, Lord!
I have felt you throbbing
in the perfect stillness
of a little Alpine church,
in the shadow of the tabernacle
of an empty cathedral,
in the breathing as one soul
of a crowd who love you and who fill
the arches of your church
with songs and love.
I have found you in joy,
I have spoken to you
beyond the starry firmament,
when in the evening, in silence,
I was returning home from work.
I seek you and often I find you.
But where I *always* find you
is in suffering.
A suffering, any sort of suffering,
is like the sound of a bell
that summons God's bride to prayer.
When the shadow of the cross appears
the soul recollects itself
in the tabernacle of its heart
and, forgetting the tinkling of the bell,
it sees you and speaks to you.
It is you who come to visit me.
It is I who answer you:
'Here I am, Lord, I desire you, I have desired you.'
And in this meeting
my soul does not feel its suffering,
but is as if inebriated with your love;
suffused with you, imbued with you;
I in you and you in me,
that we may be one.
And then I re-open my eyes to life,

to the life less real,
divinely trained
to wage your war.

From the Focolare Movement

Prayer of St Ephraim the Syrian

O Lord and Master of my life,
Grant not to me a spirit of laziness, of despondency,
Of lust of power or of gossiping.

Prostration

But grant to me, your servant,
The spirit of purity, of humility,
Of patience and of love.

Prostration

Yes, O Lord and King,
Grant that I may see my own errors and transgressions
And not judge my brother,
For blessed are you, to the ages of ages.
Amen.

Prostration

O God, cleanse me, a sinner.

*This line is repeated 12 times, with the sign of the cross and a bow each time.
Then the whole prayer is said once more, with one final prostration.*

From the Community of St Fursey

Who consoles their weeping?

Give me all who are lonely ... I have felt in my heart the passion that fills
your heart for all the forsakeness in which the whole of the world is drifting.
I love everyone who is sick and alone.
Who consoles their weeping?
Who mourns their slow death?

Who presses to their own heart, the heart in despair?
My God, let me be in this world the tangible sacrament of your love; let me
be your arms that press to themselves and consume in love all the
loneliness of the world.

From the Focolare Community

Make us ready for your kingdom

Father,
forgive us,
purify us,
make us ready for your kingdom.
We know we are in great need
of forgiveness,
in great need
for your Son Jesus to come
and lay his hands
on each of us
and make us new.
Give us this power
of forgiveness.
Amen.

From the Darvell Bruderhof

Passion Week

Ride on in majesty

The words in bold may be said all together.

Lord Jesus Christ,
…over the broken glass of our world,
the rumours meant to hurt,
the prejudice meant to wound,
the weapons meant to kill,
ride on …
trampling our attempts at disaster into the dust.
    Ride on,
    ride on in majesty.

…over the distance
which separates us from you,
and it is such a distance,
measurable in half-truths,
in unkept promises
in second-best obedience,
ride on …
until you touch and heal us,
who feel for no one but ourselves.
    Ride on,
    ride on in majesty.

…through the back streets
and the sin bins
and the sniggered-at corners of the city,
where human life festers
and love runs cold,
ride on …
bringing hope and dignity
where most send scorn and silence.
    Ride on,
    ride on in majesty.

For you, O Christ, do care
and must show us how.
On our own,
our ambitions rival your summons
and thus threaten good faith
and neglect God's people.

In your company and at your side,
we might yet help to bandage and heal
the wounds of the world.
>**Ride on,**
>**ride on in majesty,**
>**and take us with you.**
>**Amen.**
>> *From the Iona Community*

Holy Week

Beloved, once more, on my knees, I face another day. My heart is heavy, for it is Holy Week, the week of your crucifixion. As I follow your passion with you, my heart seems to break, and tears come to my eyes. Jesus, Son of God, come down to save us sinners, and have mercy on me, the greatest sinner of them all.

This week, my life, in comparison to your passion, leaves me aghast. True, I weep. But I ask you more: grant to me, this Holy Week, the light to better understand the enormity of sin, the infinity of your love, the greatness of your mercy; and, having understood better, to run to do my work.

Let your words, 'I am thirsty', echo and re-echo in my soul, never allowing me any rest. Souls! You want souls! Let me – by practising the works of mercy, by loving you, by living in you – let me, I beg you, bring souls to you. Alone, I know I cannot do anything. But with you and through you, I can.

O Jesus, Beloved, I want to be with you everywhere throughout your passion. But, above all, I want to be at the foot of the cross. May I? Like Magdalene? I have sinned much, but you have forgotten much. My place is with you in reparation. O Beloved, I love, love, love you. Give me the light and strength to love you more and more.

From the Madonna House Community

Out of ourselves

Jesus, give as your Holy Spirit,
Who pulls us out of ourselves
And out of all self-life
And self-will
And makes us willing
To die for you,
To give our lives for you.
Abba, Father in heaven,
Father of Jesus Christ and our Father,
We want to declare our readiness
To be mocked and degraded
And made small,
If only we are allowed to be yours,
To endure to the end.
Amen.

From the Darvell Bruderhof

Holy Thursday

Holy Thursday Supper

This liturgy is based on the Jewish celebration of the Passover. It takes place in the context of a meal, with unleavened bread, bitter herbs, haroset and wine.

Candles are lit.

Leader   Blessed are you, Lord, God of all creation,
for giving us your commandments
and commanding us to kindle lights on this festival.
Blessed are you, Lord, God of all creation,
for keeping us alive and letting us come here
to take part in this feast.
May the Lord bless you and keep you all this night.
May the Lord make his face shine upon you
and be gracious to you.
May the Lord turn his face towards you
and give you peace.

The leader raises the unleavened bread.

Leader   This is the bread of suffering,
the humble and simple bread
which our fathers ate in the land of Egypt.
Come in, hungry stranger, and eat with us.
Come in, homeless wanderer, and celebrate the Passover in our home.
This year many peoples throughout the world
are persecuted and oppressed –
next year may they be happy and free.
Next year may we all keep a joyful Passover in the Kingdom of God.

The servers lay a place for the unexpected guest.

A child   Why is this night different from every other night in the year?

Leader	Through his servant, Moses, the God of our fathers
	brought the children of Israel out of Egypt
	and gave them a land flowing with milk and honey.
	Blessed is the Lord, who keeps his promise to his people.
	Year after year we gather together to retell this story.
	For it is not really ancient,
	but in its message and spirit
	it applies to the history of God's people in every age.

A bowl of water and a towel are passed around for us to wash our hands.

Reader	O give thanks to the Lord, for he is good.
All	**Great is his love, love without end.**

Reader	O give thanks to the God of gods.
All	**Great is his love, love without end.**

Reader	O give thanks to the Lord of lords.
All	**Great is his love, love without end.**

Reader	To him who alone does great wonders.
All	**Great is his love, love without end.**

Leader	A full cup is a symbol of complete joy.
	We celebrate our liberation, but our happiness is not complete.
	All people are the children of God, even our enemies.
	We do not rejoice over the downfall of the Egyptians.
	We show our sorrow over the losses which each of the plagues caused.

The leader drips four drops from a cup into a saucer.

Leader	Blood, frogs, gnats, flies, plague, boils, hail, locusts, darkness, death of the first-born.

Reader	He brought Israel out from among them.
All	**Great is his love, love without end.**

Reader	With a strong hand and an outstretched arm.
All	**Great is his love, love without end.**

Reader	He divided the Red Sea in sunder.
All	**Great is his love, love without end.**

Reader	And made Israel pass through the midst of it.
All	**Great is his love, love without end.**

A child	Why do we eat unleavened bread on this night?

Leader	The flat unleavened bread is in memory of the flight of our ancestors from Eygpt, when there was no time for the dough to rise.

A child	Why do we eat bitter herbs?

Leader	The bitter herbs remind us of the bitterness of slavery, when our ancestors' lives were embittered by forced labour and oppression.

A child	Why do we eat haroset?

Leader	We eat the haroset to remind us of the mortar with which our ancestors made bricks for the building of Egyptian cities.
	In every generation it is the duty of all of us to regard ourselves as though we personally were among those who came out of Egypt. Not only our fathers did the Holy One, blessed be he, redeem from suffering. He also redeemed us and our families.

The leader breaks the unleavened bread and gives a piece to each participant.

Leader	Blessed are you, Lord, who sanctified us by commandments and commanded us to eat bitter herbs.

We each put a small portion of bitter herbs and sweet haroset on our bread, as a sign that we believe in God's goodness in bringing good to triumph over evil.

All	**Blessed are you, Lord, God of all creation.**
	Through your goodness we have this bread to eat,
	which earth has given and human hands have made.

We eat the bread as the beginning of the Passover meal, which we now enjoy together. After the meal the leader says:

Leader	We are about to drink the cup of wine in gratitude for the freedom which the Lord granted to our ancestors, and in thankfulness for earth's gifts, of which we have eaten.

All	Blessed are you, Lord, God of all creation.
	Through your goodness we have this wine to drink,
	fruit of the vine and work of human hands.

We drink from the wine.

| Leader | Now that the Passover service is complete and we have told the ancient story of Israel's liberation, and shared the traditional foods, let us sing together a final hymn. |

All	Shalom, my friend, Shalom, my friend,
	Shalom, Shalom.
	The peace of Christ I give you today,
	Shalom, Shalom.

Leader	May it be God's will
	to preserve us in life and good health
	to celebrate together again next year.
All	Next year in the New Jerusalem.

From the Hengrave Community

The washing of the feet

This liturgy is particularly suitable for Maundy Thursday, and could follow a Passover meal. It may be used by large groups of people who do not know each other well. Smaller groups may equally celebrate it more informally. The words in bold are said all together.

The celebrants enter, with two people carrying a Bible.

| Celebrant | When Jesus had washed their feet and put on his outer garments again, he went back to the table. 'Do you understand,' he said, 'what I have done to you? You call me Teacher and Lord, and you are right, so I am. If I, then, the Lord and Teacher, have washed your feet, you ought to wash one another's feet. I have given you an example, that you also should do as I have done to you.' |
| All sing | Veni, Sancte Spiritus. |

| Celebrant | But now in Christ Jesus you who once were far off have been brought near by the blood of Christ. |
| All | Christ is our peace. |

Celebrant	Christ makes us one, and has broken down the dividing wall of hostility.
All	**Christ is our peace.**

Celebrant	He emptied himself, taking the form of a servant.
All	**Christ is our peace.**

Celebrant	In a world that empties human life of meaning, we are called to a vision of humanity restored to fullness through welcome and covenant.
All	**Christ is our peace.**

Celebrant	In a world devoured by despair, we are called to live and proclaim the good news.
All	**Christ is our peace.**

Celebrant	In a world where many forces deter us from obeying the voice of Christ, we are called to be faithful to our call and our covenant.
All	**Christ is our peace.**

Celebrant	In a world of division and discord, we are called to oneness.
All	**Christ is our peace.**

Silence. This is followed by the prayer of confession below.

Celebrant	Almighty God, we have sinned against you, our neighbours, all humanity and the whole created order. We have let pride, negligence, ignorance and wilful disobedience get in the way of your love. We have closed our hearts to those around us, especially to the weak and the poor. We have allowed our differences to mar our relationship with you and with each other. We have hurt one another in thought, word and deed. We have denied our need for transformation and change.
	For all the suffering and pain that indifference, resentment and prejudice have caused,
All	**Kyrie Eleison.**

Celebrant	For the pride which has prevented forgiveness, understanding and openness to each other,
All	**Kyrie Eleison.**

Celebrant	For the times we were blind and failed to see the beauty in the other, For the times we were deaf and failed to listen to the other, For the times we were dumb and failed to talk with the other, For the times we failed to recognise our covenant with each other as a gift from you,
All	**Kyrie Eleison.**
Celebrant	For the violence we do to each other which spills into our world,
All	**Kyrie Eleison.**
Celebrant	For our greed and selfishness that cause many to face this and every night alone, hopeless, homeless, insecure, hungry, fearful, confused or locked up in institutions,
All	**Kyrie Eleison.**
Celebrant	So if anyone is in Christ, there is a new creation: everything old has passed away; see, everything has become new! All this is from God, who reconciled us to himself through Christ, and has given us the ministry of reconciliation; that is, in Christ, God was reconciling the world to himself, not counting their trespasses against them, and entrusting the message of reconciliation to us.
Readings	*Isaiah 58:6-12* *Philippians 2:5-11*
All sing	**Alleluia.**
The Gospel	*John 13:1-17*
All sing	**Alleluia.**
Homily	
Celebrant	And now we will make the profession of Christian faith into which we were baptised and in which we live and grow. Do you believe and trust in God, the Father who made the world?
All	**I believe in God, the Father almighty, creator of heaven and earth.**

Celebrant	Do you believe and trust in his Son Jesus Christ, who redeemed humankind?
All	**I believe in Jesus Christ, his only Son our Lord, who was conceived by the power of the Holy Spirit and born of the Virgin Mary. He suffered under Pontius Pilate, was crucified, died and was buried; he descended to the dead. On the third day he rose again. He ascended into heaven, and is seated at the right hand of the Father. He will come again to judge the living and the dead.**

Celebrant	Do you believe and trust in his Holy Spirit, who gives life to the people of God?
All	**I believe in the Holy Spirit, the holy universal Church, the communion of saints, the forgiveness of sins, the resurrection of the body, and life everlasting. Amen.**

Celebrant	This is the faith of the Church.
All	**This is our faith. We believe and trust in one God, Father, Son and Holy Spirit.**

Different people may read the intercessions below.

| Reader | Today Christians from different Churches
cannot eat around the same table of the broken bread,
transformed into the body of Christ;
but we can eat together around the table
which welcomes the broken, the poor and the weak.
Today Christians from different Churches
cannot drink from the same chalice of the blood of Christ;
but they and all our brothers and sisters in Christ
can drink together
from the same chalice of suffering, of division, of anguish
in our Church, our country and in our world.
Together we can pour out the sweet oil of compassion
upon the wounds of humanity.
We pray that unity will come. |
|---|---|
| All | **Amen, come, Lord Jesus!** |

Reader	Come through the treasure of your holy word, sharper than a two-edged sword that pierces into us, cleansing us from all shame and deceit.
All	**Amen, come, Lord Jesus!**

Reader	Come through the treasure of your body broken, risen, strengthening, nurturing, that we know in the Eucharist.
All	**Amen, come, Lord Jesus!**

Celebrant	Come through the treasure of our own weakness, vulnerability and pain.
	Come through all our brothers and sisters.
	Come through our differences and in those we see as enemies.
All	**Amen, come, Lord Jesus!**

Celebrant	Come, then, as you came among your disciples to wash their feet; send your Holy Spirit upon us that we who seek your grace may live by its power.
All	**Amen, come, Lord Jesus!**

There may be singing.
At this point members of communities may wish to renew the covenant which they have with Jesus and their brothers and sisters.

Celebrant	All-powerful and ever-living God,
	we do well always and everywhere to give you thanks,
	through Jesus Christ our Lord.
	You sent your Son to live among us,
	so that we might learn from him humility and obedience.
	His nature was divine,
	yet he did not cling to his equality with God,
	but emptied himself to assume the condition of a slave.
	He became as we are, and was humbler yet,
	accepting death, even death on a cross.
	But you, Father, raised him high,
	and gave him a name which is above all names,
	so that we can acclaim,
	Jesus is Lord,
	to your honour and glory,
	and join with the whole company of heaven and earth, saying:
	Holy, holy, holy Lord,
	God of power and might,
	heaven and earth are full of your glory.
	Hosanna in the highest.
	Blessed is he who comes in the name of the Lord.
	Hosanna in the highest.
	Ever-loving God,
	we thank you for the great gift of Jesus, your Son,

for the example he gave us of love and service,
for his promise to be with those who love and follow him.
Having loved his own, he loved them to the end.
On the night before he gave his life for us,
knowing that you had put everything into his hands,
he met with his disciples
and gave them his new commandment:

All   **'Love one another as I have loved you.'**

Celebrant   Getting up from table, he took a towel and water, washing the
disciples' feet, and said:

All   **'I have given you an example.
You are to do for one another what I have done for you.'**

Celebrant   As we remember Jesus, his life, his love even unto death,
his desire for our unity in his love.
his resurrection,
we rejoice that he has given us his Spirit
to be his hands and body now in the world.

May the Holy Spirit create in us the mind that was in Christ
Jesus
to enable us to love and live as he did,
without counting the cost,
to desire a unity in love as he did,
without losing heart.

All   **Heal the broken body of humanity,
the broken body of your Church.**

Celebrant   Father, we know ourselves to be weak and vulnerable;
we too are poor, but it is in our poverty and brokenness
that you come to us, and reveal the depths of your love.

For all this we give you thanks
through Jesus Christ your Son
who lives and reigns with you and the Holy Spirit,
one God for ever and ever. **Amen.**

*The group leaders begin by each washing the feet of one of their neighbours.
Those whose feet have been washed then place their hands on the heads of
those who have washed their feet. They pray silently together. Then those who
have had their feet washed each wash the feet of a person next to them. And so*

on, until the last people wash the feet of the group leaders. When all is complete, a song is sung, followed by the Our Father, said by each person in his or her own language.

Celebrant	May the Lord bless you and keep you.
All	**Amen.**

Celebrant	May the Lord let his face shine on you and be gracious to you.
All	**Amen.**

Celebrant	May the Lord God uncover his face to you and bring you peace.
All	**Amen.**

Celebrant	Let's give each other a sign of peace.

From L'Arche Lambeth

Good Friday

From the wood of the crib

A silent tableau may be created by three people, representing Jesus, with Mary and John, who stay standing at the foot of the cross. A wooden cross and crib complete the scene.

From the wood of the crib
To the wood of the cross,
All the grief of creation
Is entombed in loss:
The temple's veil now
Torn, torn asunder,
With a covenant love
Of water that flows with blood.

From the wood of the crib
To the wood of the cross,
With the sky torn by darkness,
All their hopes felt lost:
But John is given
Mary, his mother,
With a covenant love
Of water that flows with blood.

From the womb of the crib
To the womb of the cross,
All the hope of creation
Will transfigure loss:
Her heart still ponders
Birthplace of wonder,
Holds a covenant love
Of water that flows with blood.

From the womb of the crib
To the womb of the cross,
At the heart of creation
Beat these words of loss:

Behold, your mother,
Mother, your son who
Holds a covenant love
Of water that flows with blood.
From L'Arche Edinburgh

The Reproaches

This liturgy may be part of a service held at 3 p.m., the time of Christ's death.

Reader   My people, what have I done to you?
How have I offended you, answer me.

All   **Holy God, holy and strong, holy and immortal, have mercy on us.**

Reader   For forty years I led you safely through the desert,
I fed you with manna from heaven
and brought you to a land of plenty,
but you led your Saviour to the cross.

What more could I have done for you?
I planted you as my fairest vine, but you yielded only bitterness.
When I was thirsty, you gave me vinegar to drink
and you pierced your Saviour's side with a lance.

All   **Holy God, holy and strong, holy and immortal, have mercy on us.**

Reader   For your sake I scourged your captors and their firstborn sons,
but you brought your scourges down on me.
My people, what have I done to you?
How have I offended you? Answer me.

I led you from slavery to freedom,
and drowned your captors in the sea,
but you handed me over to your high priests.
I opened the sea before you,
but you opened my side with a spear.
My people, what have I done to you? Answer me.

I led you on your way in a pillar of cloud,
but you led me to Pilate's court.
I bore you up with manna in the desert,
but you struck me down and scourged me.

All   **Holy God, holy and strong, holy and immortal, have mercy on us.**

Reader   I gave you saving water from the rock,
but you gave me gall and vinegar to drink.
For you I struck down the kings of Canaan,
but you struck my head with a reed.
My people, what have I done to you? Answer me.
I gave you a royal sceptre,
but you gave me a crown of thorns.
I raised you to the height of majesty,
but you have raised me high on a cross.

All   **Holy God, holy and strong, holy and immortal, have mercy on us.**

From the Hengrave Community

Cross-carrying Jesus

Cross-carrying Jesus,
as you stagger on your lonely journey
time slips
worlds reel.
Forgive us that we turn away
embarrassed
uncaring
despairing.
Help us to stay with you
through the dark night
to watch and to wait
to know the depths of your anguish
and to realise that you carry us,
forgive (even) us,
love us.
Forgive us
that we get on with our work unthinking
that we gamble unknowing with precious things.

Cross-carrying Jesus,
nailed to the tree of life,
forgive us
and grant us your salvation.

From the Iona Community

Jesus, the clown prince of sorrows

A group activity could include making a scarecrow together, followed by a time of prayer with a wordless tableau created by one person as Jesus on the cross, some passers-by, and the remorseful thief to his right. Two voices slowly read the meditation.

Jesus, the clown prince of sorrows,
Hung like a scarecrow despised.
A lottery's gift his clothing –
Status and power put by.
Nobody knows their meaning,
Each follows words from those on high.
The king of God's people tortured,
Broken, betrayed by a spy.
Jesus, the clown prince of sorrows,
Hung like a scarecrow despised.
The passers-by mock at weakness,
Make fun of power put by.

> O Abba, Father, hear me,
> Why have you left your son to die?
> Beelzebul's vision is over –
> Out of the depths comes my cry.

> Struck by your plea to remember,
> Hearing remorse in your cry,
> The day of the dead before us,
> Yet I will bear you on high.
> Mercy for all to hope in,
> Brings you to welcome God's embrace.
> And those who despise and torture –
> Father, forgive them their sin.

Jesus, the clown prince of sorrows,
Hung like a scarecrow despised.

From L'Arche Edinburgh

The silence of the cross

In this silence
Lord
I gaze upon your cross.
The frenzied words
of hate and venom
hurled at you
with wild abandon
by your despisers
have now subsided.
The shrieks
and taunting jeers
have now died down
as your life
ebbs quietly away.
The deafening, mocking cries
are now displaced
by this deadly
stillness,
awesome
burdensome
shameful
and now
in this unpeaceful quietness
I look at you
and what I see
overwhelms me
and brings me
to the point
beyond all tears
beyond all words
beyond all thoughts
where I begin
to understand
the full magnitude
of what we have done to you
of what you have done
for me.

From the Maranatha Community

Eastertide

The Exultet

This liturgy may be used at an Easter Eve vigil.

Reader   Rejoice, heavenly powers! Sing, choirs of angels!
Exult, all creation around God's throne!
Jesus Christ, our King, is risen!
Sound the trumpet of salvation!

Rejoice, O earth, in shining splendour,
radiant in the brightness of your King!
Christ has conquered! Glory fills you!
Darkness vanishes for ever!

Rejoice, O Mother Church! Exult in glory!
The risen Saviour shines upon you!
Let this place resound with joy,
echoing the mighty song of all God's people!

Leader   The Lord be with you.
All   **And also with you.**

Leader   Lift up your hearts.
All   **We lift them up to the Lord.**

Leader   Let us give thanks to the Lord our God.
All   **It is right to give him thanks and praise.**

Reader   It is truly right
that with full hearts and minds and voices
we should praise the unseen God, the all-powerful Father,
and his only Son, our Lord Jesus Christ.

For Christ has ransomed us with his blood,
and paid for us the price of Adam's sin
to our eternal Father!

This is our Passover feast,
when Christ, the true Lamb, is slain,
whose blood consecrates the homes of all believers.

This is the night when first you saved our fathers:
you freed the people of Israel from their slavery
and led them dry-shod through the sea.

This is the night when Christians everywhere,
washed clean of sin
and freed from all defilement,
are restored to grace and grow together in holiness.

This is the night when Jesus Christ
broke the chains of death
and rose triumphant from the grave.

Father, how wonderful your care for us!
How boundless your merciful love!
To ransom a slave
you gave away your Son.

O happy fault, O necessary sin of Adam,
which gained for us so great a Redeemer!

The power of this holy night
dispels all evil, washes sin away,
restores lost innocence, brings mourners joy.

Night truly blessed when heaven is wedded to earth
and humanity is reconciled with God!

Therefore, heavenly Father, in the joy of this night,
receive our evening sacrifice of praise,
your Church's solemn offering.

Accept this Easter candle.
May it always dispel the darkness of this night!

May the Morning Star which never sets find this flame still
     burning:
Christ, the Morning Star, who came back from the dead,

and shed his peaceful light on all humankind,
your Son who lives and reigns for ever and ever.

All   **Amen.**

From the Hengrave Community

Christ is risen!

Beloved, I love you. I adore you. I thank you. Because of your death, we have life. Because of your Resurrection, we have faith.

O Jesus, beloved Friend, Master, I believe, I love, I thank, I adore. Teach me to always keep your peace, to always walk before your face, to always remember your great commandment: 'Love one another as I have loved you.'

Beloved, my heart overflows with love and gratitude. I have only my heart to offer. Here it is. You fashioned it; you made it. It is yours as I am yours: memory, will, intellect, body, soul, heart, all my faculties. Beloved, keep me in your heart, for I was made for you.

From the Madonna House Community

Pentecost

Prayer to the Holy Spirit

Come into me, O Holy Spirit.

Grant to me your understanding, so that I may know the Father by meditating on the Gospel.

Grant to me your wisdom, so that I may know how to relive and judge, in the light of your Word, that which I have seen today.

Grant to me perseverance, so that with patience I may penetrate the message of God in the Gospel, and take from there the illumination in order to love life and the Lord of life.

Grant to me your trust, so that I may know how to be from now on in mysterious communion with God, waiting to be immersed in him in eternal life, where his Word will be finally unveiled and fully realised.

From the Dominican Sisters of St Joseph

Light and fire

Light and fire on the face of Christ,
Fire that brings the Word;
Fire of silence and light;
Fire filling our hearts with thanksgiving,
We give you praise.

You who rested on Christ,
Spirit of knowledge and wisdom,
Spirit of counsel and strength,
Spirit of love and fear,
We give you praise.

You who reach the depths of God,
You who give light to our hearts,
Spirit praying within us,

Spirit in whom we reflect the glory of the Lord,
We give you praise.

> *From the Hengrave Community*

Come, Holy Spirit

Come, Holy Spirit, reign in me.
Come, Holy Spirit, set me free.
Fill my heart with your love.
Make me more like Jesus.

> *From the Pilgrims Community*

The Transfiguration

Chew on the gospels

This prayer may be said by two voices or groups. It may also be expanded into a simple mime, with two people as disciples responding to the text's injunctions: chewing, listening, fighting-then-forgiving; receiving bread from a third figure who enters in scene two; piling up possessions and then being encouraged to give them away; and finally going on their way in joy, sent by the figure of Jesus, who remains in the centre, holding a flat bowl or plate in which a pile of ash is visible.

Chew on the gospels,
Let their word transform our lives,
Let all we do be with God's breath inspired.
Listen to God,
Obey the word of Jesus,
Holding to love,
So learning to forgive.

    Find help on the way of transfiguration,
    Trust in God, who hears our cry for bread.

Value the food from bread that's blessed and broken,
Welcoming those who lack the means to give,
See that we don't
Pile up yet more possessions,
Ask for the gift of humour in our lives.

    Find help on the way of transfiguration,
    Trust in God, who hears our cry for bread.

All we endure will count as much as all we do,
Offer ourselves, a gift of love and praise,
Go on our way with songs of jubilation.
Pray for the dead
Of human genocide.

    Find help on the way of transfiguration,

Trust in God, who hears our cry for bread,
Who hears our cry for bread.
From L'Arche Edinburgh

High over all

They rank you with the others,
Lord –
teachers,
gurus
and guides.
They place you with the others,
Lord –
the gentle,
kindly,
good.
They nod approvingly
and patronise your name
and speak of your words
of peace
and love
and fuse them
with all other words
spoken from many lips,
and lose you
amidst the babble
of many voices,
the confusion
of the centuries,
submerging you,
locking you away,
affirming your humanity,
not willing to see you
as you really are:
unique
without an equal
standing apart
from all others
special
supreme
the one
whose name

is above all others
God's presence with us.

From the Maranatha Community

Prayer of the heart

My eyes, my eyes
have seen the King.
The vision of his beauty
has pierced me deep within.
To whom else can I go?

My heart, my heart
desires him.
He's touched something inside of me
that's now reaching out for him.
And I know that I must go.

My God is my love,
my guard, my healing one;
my bright love
is my merciful Lord;
My sweet love is Christ;
his heart is my delight;
all my love are you,
O King of glory.
Amen.

From the Northumbria Community

All Souls and dying

The coming of death

Indeed, Beloved, I know not when you will come. But, daily, my desire for your arrival grows. I used to be afraid of death. But now, since I have realised that it is just the last step to you, I welcome death. O Beloved, it is easy to face death knowing you will be there to meet me. But it is not easy for me to pray for death, as I want time to put my whole life into your hands.

Now there is this life. I want it to be all for you. I want it to be such that I would be ready for you at all times. Take me now, all of me, as St Ignatius says, 'my memory, my understanding, my entire will', for everything has been given to me by you, Beloved.

Often, I want to shout and thank you and sing for sheer joy and happiness when I realise all you have given me: the grace to love you, the desire to serve you, membership in your Church, a love of the poor, friendships that light up my life, and, daily, yourself, O Jesus. Thank you, Beloved, thank you.

From the Madonna House Community

Walking with grief

Do not hurry
as you walk with grief;
it does not help the journey.

Walk slowly,
pausing often;
do not hurry
as you walk with grief.

Be not disturbed
by memories that come unbidden.
Swiftly forgive;
and let Christ speak for you
unspoken words.
Unfinished conversation

will be resolved in him.
Be not disturbed.

Be gentle with the one
who walks with grief.
If it is you,
be gentle with yourself.
Swiftly forgive;
walk slowly,
pausing often.

Take time, be gentle
as you walk with grief.

From the Northumbria Community

The long vigil

Lord Jesus,
there are times when we are faced with sorrow,
when we go through the long vigil
with someone who suffers and dies;
when we see the pain and hunger
of an oppressed people.
Your disciples experienced sorrow
when you were taken from them.
But the sorrow of the evening went
in the joy of the resurrection morning.
Help us to believe
that one day all wrongs will be righted,
all pain and suffering will be ended,
that you will be one with your people
in an abundant feast of joy.

From the Community for Reconciliation

Beyond our boundaries

God of all creation –
who cannot be contained by our boundaries
or our definitions –
light from beyond the galaxies,
sea without a farther shore,

you are present in every distinct place,
in every moment in history.
You are here and now.
Help us to understand
that those from whom we are separated
by difference, by prejudice,
by language, by lack of communication;
and those from whom we are separated in death,
by its long silence, its aching absence –
are each of them in your presence:
that beyond our horizons,
beyond our boundaries,
beyond our understanding,
they are in your embrace. Amen.

From the Iona Community

As if it were the last day

Lord,
Help me to say every word
as if were my last.
Help me to carry out every deed
as if it were my last act.
Help me to suffer always
as if it were the last suffering I have
to offer to you.
Help me to pray always
as if it were the last chance
I have here on earth
to speak to you.

From the Focolare Movement

Ordinary Time

Day by day

Radiating Christ

Dear Jesus, help me to spread your fragrance
everywhere I go.
Flood my soul with your Spirit and life.

Penetrate and possess my whole being, so utterly
that my life may be only a radiance of yours.

Shine through me, and be so in me,
that every soul I come in contact with
may feel your presence in my soul.

Let them look up and see no longer me but only Jesus!
Stay with me, and then I shall begin to shine as you shine;

So to shine as to be a light to others; the light,
O Jesus, will be all from you, none of it will be mine;
it will be you, shining on others through me.

Let me praise you in the way you love best –
by shining on those around me.

Let me preach you without preaching,
not by words, but by example, by the catching force,

the sympathetic influence of what I do,
the evident fulness of the love my heart bears to you.
Amen.
From Youth 2000

To be faithful in little things

Jesus, we all dream of big, heroic actions for your sake. Teach us to be ready
for them if they come. But show me the value of little, daily, humble things
done well. Teach me to understand the depth of the saying, 'Because you have
been faithful in little things . . .' It may only be a word suppressed, a smile

given, a weakness overcome. These small acts, too, can win heaven for some-one. Teach me to do them. Teach me to remember the thirty years of hidden life you lived before the three public years of your miracles. Let me see the beauty of small hidden things done out of love for you. Jesus, teach me the greatness of little things.

From the Madonna House Community

The Master Carpenter

O Christ the Master Carpenter, who at the last through wood and nails purchased our whole salvation, wield well your tools in the workshop of your world, so that we who come rough-hewn to your bench may here be fashioned to a truer beauty of your hand. We ask it for your own name's sake. Amen.

From the Iona Community

In the heart of God

This may be sung to the tune of 'Exaltabo te' by J. Berthier, Taizé.

In the heart of God, only goodness;
In a human heart, cry of longing.
In the heart of God, only goodness;
In a human heart, cry of longing.
In a covenant with the joiner's son
God the Spirit comes, alleluia.
In the heart of God, cry of mercy;
In a human heart, only longing.

From L'Arche Edinburgh

To do all things with your blessing

O Jesus, I have learned that only when I do your will in all things and start everything with your blessing do I find in my actions happiness and peace – your peace.

Help me, Lord, always in all things – to do them with you, to pray over them, to ask your blessing, and to keep before my eyes the pure intention of loving you and doing all things for that love and your greater glory. Amen.

From the Madonna House Community

Goodness is stronger

The verses in bold may be said all together.

Because you made the world,
and intended it to be a good place,
and called its people your children;
because, when things seemed at their worst,
you came in Christ to bring out the best in us;
so, gracious God, we gladly say:

Goodness is stronger than evil,
Love is stronger than hate,
Light is stronger than darkness,
Truth is stronger than lies.

Because confusion can reign inside us,
despite our faith;
because anger, tension, bitterness and envy
distort our vision;
because our minds sometimes worry about small things
out of all proportion;
because we do not always get it right,
we want to believe:

Goodness is stronger than evil,
Love is stronger than hate,
Light is stronger than darkness,
Truth is stronger than lies.

Because you have promised to hear us,
and are able to change us,
and are willing to make our hearts your home,
we ask you to confront,
control, forgive and encourage us,
as you know best.

Pause.

Then let us cherish in our hearts
that which we proclaim with our lips:

**Goodness is stronger than evil,
Love is stronger than hate,
Light is stronger than darkness,
Truth is stronger than lies.**

Lord, hear our prayer,
and change our lives
until we illustrate the grace
of the God who makes all things new.

Amen.

From the Iona Community

A heart set free

Give me, O Lord, an ever-watchful heart
which no subtle speculation
may ever lure from you.

Give me a noble heart
that no unworthy affection
shall ever draw downwards to earth.

Give me a heart of honesty
that no insincerity shall warp.

Give me a heart of courage
that no distress shall ever crush or quench.

Give me a heart so free
that no perverted or impetuous affection
shall ever claim for its own.

From the Dominican Sisters of St Joseph

Signs of dawn

O God, you have set before us a great hope that your kingdom will come on earth, and have taught us to pray for its coming; make us ever ready to thank you for the signs of its dawning, and to pray and work for the perfect day when your will shall be done on earth as it is in heaven. Through Jesus Christ our Lord. Amen.

From the Iona Community

A flexible wineskin

Keep us a flexible wineskin, God,
That we may give others who come to us room,
And not force them into our mould,
That we may grow together.

From the Daily Bread Co-operative

Tell me

Tell me, Lord,
and keep on
telling me
that
without you
I can do
nothing –
absolutely
and
completely
nothing.

From the Maranatha Community

Only small things

We can do no great things –
only small things with great love.

From the Missionaries of Charity

Praise and adoration

Bless the Lord

Reader Round church tower in changing light,
Chasing shadows, bless the Lord,
Pascal fire, flaming all night,
Still white candle, bless the Lord.

All **At all times we'll bless the Lord,
Bless his holy name.**

Reader Pollarded limes, stabbing the mist,
Skein of geese, bless the Lord,
Water, darkling or sunkissed,
Icy flagstones, bless the Lord.

All **At all times we'll bless the Lord,
Bless his holy name.**

Reader Hedges, lawns and leaning yews,
Archways, gateways, bless the Lord,
Sunrise, sunset which suffuse
Walls and windows, bless the Lord.

All **At all times we'll bless the Lord,
Bless his holy name.**

Reader Scuttling hens and cocks that crow
Trees in blossom, bless the Lord,
All that wakes and sways and grows,
Spring-time, ring-time, bless the Lord.

All **At all times we'll bless the Lord,
Bless his holy name.**

Reader Ox-eyed daisies, windfalls, hay,
Apple-peeling, bless the Lord,
Bees a-hum, some summer days,
Rose-petal wine, bless the Lord.

All **At all times we'll bless the Lord,
Bless his holy name.**

Reader	Maples, shumachs copper-tinted,
	Autumn glory, bless the Lord,
	Beeches, chestnuts, winter-stripped,
	Frost-rimmed pool, bless the Lord.
All	**At all times we'll bless the Lord,**
	Bless his holy name.

Reader	Whistling wind and scudding cloud,
	Sudden lightning, bless the Lord,
	Woods before the storm-burst bowed,
	Sudden stillness, bless the Lord.
All	**At all times we'll bless the Lord,**
	Bless his holy name.

From the Hengrave Community

Gratitude

I love you
not because I have learned to tell you so,
not because my heart
suggests these words to me,
not even because faith
makes me believe that you are love,
nor even simply
because you died for me.

I love you
because you have entered my life
more than the air in my lungs,
more than the blood in my veins.
You entered
where no one else could enter,
where no one could help me,
every time no one
could console me.

Every day I have spoken to you.
Every hour I have looked at you,
and in your face

I have read the answer,
in your words
the explanation,
in your love
the solution.

I love you
because for many years
you have lived with me
and I
have lived of your life.
I have drunk of your law
without knowing it.

I have been nourished by it,
and strengthened;
I have started afresh,
but without realising it,
like a child that suckles
at its mother's breast
and does not yet know
how to call her
by that sweet name.

Let me show my gratitude to you,
at least a little,
in the time left me,
for this love
which you have lavished on me,
and which has urged me
to tell you:
I love you.

From the Focolare Movement

Jesus, be at home in my heart

O my Lord, I love you beyond anyone or anything I have ever loved or can love. I adore you. I know you dwell in my soul. And yet, I allow it to be filled with so many things besides you. I am loathe to clean house because my detachment is not complete. I am still attached to my own will, to certain people, to certain comforts. Teach me to overcome myself and them.

I realise how near you are. Your mercy shines like a light, and my sins are as if they were not. How wonderful it is to be so close to you. The birds, the flowers, the grass, the stars and heavens all speak of you. But come and make your home in me.

From the Madonna House Community

Worship

The purest worship
I can offer
is the silence
of my heart,
the inexpressable depths
of my acceptance
that you are Lord
and that any word
I utter
will be inadequate
and flawed
and often even worse
than saying nothing.
My lips quiver
my heart trembles
in the awareness
of your presence
and the knowledge
that the music
of my praise
however pure
in human ears
falls short
by far
to match
your majesty
and glorious perfection.
So, Lord, impress
upon my soul
that when I climb

the holy mount
I walk
on hallowed ground.
Before I stammer
my frail unworthy words
or sing my
fragile songs of praise
give to me
a sense of awe
and wonder
but also the
joyous certainty
that you love to hear
the feeble murmurs
of your
wayward child.

From the Maranatha Community

Focus on Jesus

As we focus on you, all your promises come true.

We will rise like eagles,
  soar on wings of faith,
    dance among the stars.

As we lift our eyes to you,
  you will carry us,
    and show us everything
      from your viewpoint.

As we delight in you,
  you will give us our heart's desires.

But even if you don't,
  we say, like the men in the fiery furnace,
    even if you don't bless us,
    even if you don't deliver us,
    even if the trees don't blossom,
     and there is no fruit,
    we will still praise you.

We lift our eyes to you,
   anyway.

We worship you,
   because you are.
                From the House of the Open Door

Peace

The dove

Lord, when we strive for unity, for peace, for Shalom, so often we are like a child striving to attract a bird to feed – calling loudly, waving arms to catch its attention. But the dove of peace cannot descend into a restless heart.

Grant to us, Lord, who worship here, the inner peace, the quiet mind, the stillness that enables him to settle in our hearts. Amen.

From the Hengrave Community

Peace

You say Peace
to the storms
of my life
Peace
to my troubled heart
Peace
to my turmoil
You breathe peace
into my trembling
Peace
deep into my soul
Peace
into my thinking
Peace
into my feeling
Peace
into my being
Far beyond
all knowledge
or understanding
you speak Peace
you give Peace
you are Peace.

From the Maranatha Community

Real peace is in you

Beloved, there is real peace in the world: it is in you. Who but you could give this immense inner peace that comes on soft feet to bring holy tranquillity to a heart surrounded by the noise of continual action? It's as if my soul becomes a cool, quiet temple, standing in the shade of eternal trees – alone, an oasis in a broiling sun.

O Beloved, how peaceful you are! How quiet! How tranquil! How strong! The voices of the world dissolve into silence at the threshold of a soul filled with you!

Give me your peace! I love you. Teach me your holy quiet strength. Beloved, I love you!

From the Madonna House Community

Silence

Make your home in me

This prayer service may use a number of voices.

> Enter into yourself,
> leave behind all noise and confusion.
>
> Look within yourself
> and see whether there be
> some sweet hidden place within
> where you can be free
> from noise and argument,
> where you need not be carrying on
> your disputes,
> and planning
> to have your own stubborn way.
>
> Hear the word
>   in quietness
> that you may
>   understand it.

Lord God, look into the depths of my being – look on what you have made. Look on what you love.

You see each of us as your creation, and what you see, Lord, you see with love …for you made us out of love.

Hold me in the silence of your gaze so that I also may, in the silence of this moment, see you at the heart of my being.

> If only our minds
> could be held steady,
> they would be still for a while,
> and for that short moment
> we would glimpse
> the splendour of eternity

which is forever
still.

Lord, this is the time – time to spend with you, to rest in you.

Allow me, Lord, to relax into the mystery
of being loved
of being forgiven
of being called …
and of being totally held, now, in this moment
and forever, in love.
For your love is eternal.

> He is in our very inmost hearts,
> but our hearts
> have strayed
> from him.

Lord, how often I lose my way in life,
when there is failure,
when there is doubt,
when there is rejection,
and when I don't believe in myself any more.

O Lord, I am at times lost … I lose sight of even you, Lord, but I am never out
of sight of Jesus, my Saviour, for he gazes on me with love.

In the darkness of my lostness, Lord, shine, that in finding you I may find again
my true self.

> Where so ever you are,
> where so ever you may be praying,
> he who hears you is within you,
> hidden within,
> for he who hears you
> is not merely by your side,
> and you have no need to
> go wandering about,
> no need to be reaching out to
> God
> as though you would touch
> him with your hands.
> Where so ever you are,

where so ever you may be praying,
he who hears you is within you,
hidden within.

Lord, Thomas needed to touch in order to believe. Through faith I believe you reach out to us in our humanity. Your hand touches our hearts and inflames them to love you. Under your touch our sadness and our grief are turned into hope and joy ... our striving into peace. You gently search out my inmost being ... guiding ... calming ... reassuring ... healing ... forgiving.

As I fold my hands in prayer, let my searching, grasping cease, for I know you are there, within me, gently involved in every aspect of my life. You reach out to me, so I need not reach out to you. Amen.

From the Clare Priory Community

Inconceivable

Inconceivable, extraordinary,
something that cuts an even deeper
impression on my soul
is your stillness there,
in silence, in the tabernacle.
I come to church in the morning, and I find you there.
I run to church when I love you,
and I find you there.
And each time
you say a word to me
or you rectify a feeling.
In reality you are composing from different notes a single song,
a song that my heart has learnt by heart
and that repeats to me one word alone:
eternal love.
Oh! God, you could not invent anything better!
That silence of yours
in which the din of our life is hushed,
that silent heartbeat
which absorbs every tear;
that silence ...
that silence, more sonorous than the song of angels;
that silence
which communicates the Word to the mind
and gives the divine balm to the heart;

that silence
in which every voice finds itself channelled
and every prayer feels transformed;
That mysterious presence of yours …
Life is there,
expectation is there;
there our little heart rests
before continuing, without pause,
on its way.

    From the Focolare Movement

The silence to hear your voice

Why this strange desire for quiet and prayer and meditation? I want to be very still, not even praying with my lips – just to sit at your feet, my God, and listen to the great silence in which you seem to whisper to my heart.

There are so many things I want to hear from you in that silence. Yet I must go back to the rush and turmoil of life. But, as I think of it, I see a way out. And that is to keep deep in my soul – within the rush and turmoil – that great silence and peace in which alone we poor mortals can clearly hear your quiet voice. We are so weak that alone we can do nothing, not even keep silent in our souls in order to hear your voice.

    From the Madonna House Community

A Shalom Prayer

It is suggested that this is prayed slowly and in a place of silence.

I come as myself,
Just as I am,
This moment.
My feelings, my fears,
My joys, my sadnesses.
You see me as I really am.
You know me
Through and through.
You see all,
All that I am
Or ever have been.

Every experience in my life is laid before you:

Every image I have seen,
Each touch, each sensation,
Every word I have ever heard or spoken,
Each word, each idea,
Each thought which is imprinted in my soul
And is known to you.
You know me better than my closest friend.
You know me better than I know myself.
You know …
And because of who I am,
And in spite of what I am
You love me.
I am of inestimable value to you.
You love me through and through.
Nothing, nobody can remove me from your love.
Nothing, nobody can separate me from your love
or your presence.

You knew me at the moment of my creation,
And even then you loved me.
You knew me and loved me in my mother's womb.
My nature was known to you.
You called me by my name.
You held me in your arms.
You embraced me.
You breathed upon me.
You gave me your life and your love.
You watched over me from my earliest childhood.
You were present at all times and in all places,
My unseen playmate, schoolmate, workmate,
My unseen guest at every meal.
You shared in every encounter.
You watched over me silently
Even in the long hours of the night.
You shared in every journey.
You travelled with me.
You were at the beginning of each journey.
You were my companion on the way.
Without you I lose my way,
My journey has no purpose.
I become exhausted on the way.
But you are my Alpha and Omega.
You are my way.

You are the way itself, the Way of Life.

So, Lord, I lay before you my life:
All my yesterdays,
My todays and tomorrows.
I praise and thank you for your presence in my life.
I lift up in gratitude all the goodness and all the joy.
I now offer you all my hurts, my bruises, my rejections.
I offer you all those things of which I am ashamed:
What I have said, and done, and thought,
All that has brought hurt to you and to others.
Lord, pour your cleansing streams of living water
all over me.
Make the parched deserts of my being spring to life.
Refresh me, renew me.
Lord, breathe on me afresh now
And I will receive your life.
Lord, reach out and touch me,
And I will receive your healing.
Empty me utterly of all the rubbish within me.
This moment, Lord, take away all distractions,
All temptations, all evil thoughts and desires.
Remove from me all my anxiety.
Take away every hidden fear.
Help me to know
That your perfect love casts out all fear.

Bring me now into the deep silence of your presence.
I give you my body and ask that it may become
your dwelling place.
This moment may every part of my being
be at peace.
Let my heartbeat
Be in harmony with your heartbeat.
Let every part of my body be filled with your Spirit.
Take each blood vessel.
Take every part of my nervous system.
Take each muscle, each organ, each cell.
Fill me now
With your stillness
With the reality of your living presence.

Help me now to pray – even without words.

Help me to pray with my breathing,
To breathe in of your love and your peace,
To breathe out of my pain and sadness,
To breathe in of your cleansing and forgiveness,
To breathe out of my guilt and impurity.
So in my breathing may my body and soul be at one with you,
In harmony with you,
At ease with you.
May I be still and know that you are God.
May I be still and know that you are the Lord who brings healing.

Help me to hear your still, small voice,
Lord Jesus.
May I now hear your words:
'Peace, be still.'
May all my storms subside as I accept your real presence.

As I kneel before you
I give you my heart and all my emotions,
All my deepest feelings that lie
Hidden within me.
I give you my stillness,
But I also give you the turbulence,
The cross-currents of my life,
My feelings of failure and rejection.

I give you every relationship,
Every situation in my life,
All my reactions,
All my outbursts of joy and of anger,
All my moments of elation and despair.

Lord, I give you my intellect.
I lay before you all my frail thoughts and ideas.
I give you all my searching and striving,
My grasping after truth.

I give you all my ignorance and confusion.
I give you all my questions and doubts.
I acknowledge you to be truth,
Truth in its entirety,
Total truth in all its purity,
The truth which can set me free,

In my body, my mind and my spirit,
Free from all the bondage,
Free from all the lies and deceit of the world,
Free from my own selfishness and pride and greed.
Break the chains which hold me back, Lord.
Fling open the door of my prison,
That I may pass from the darkness of this world –
my world
And walk out into the bright light of your presence.
Father, may I now feel the radiance of your love upon my life.
May I feel the warmth of your fatherly love upon me, your child.
Trusting, depending, loving,
Help me to know what joy my response brings to you.
Give me the grace in my weakness to cry, 'Abba, Father'.
Help me to know that beneath me are your everlasting arms bearing me up.

Lord Jesus, be the Lord of my life.
Be the Lord of my thoughts and feelings,
My memories and hopes.
I accept your authority over everything
I have been, am or will be.
I bow down before you.
As I see you on your Cross,
Held down by cruel nails,
I see your arms stretched out,
Seeking to embrace the whole world,
Seeking to embrace me,
Seeking to love,
Seeking to forgive,
Seeking to make whole.

I praise you that you died for me.
Help me to know that because your love for me was so great,
I too must love myself.
I must recognise
My great worth to you.

Holy Spirit,
Source of all truth, giver of power,
Come upon me now
As gently as a dove
Or like tongues of living fire,
As quietly as a summer breeze,

Or as a mighty, roaring wind.
Come and dwell within me.
Enable me now to do those things which before were impossible.
Unworthy as I am,
Holy Spirit of the living God,
Give me those gifts which I can use to your honour and glory,
That I may show forth your fruit
Even in my life.

Glory be to you, Father.
Glory be to you, Lord Jesus Christ.
Glory be to you, Holy Spirit.
Amen.

From the Maranatha Community

Times

Morning Prayer

A family prayer

The lines in bold may be said all together.

O Lord open our lips.
> **And our mouths shall proclaim your praise.**

Let us worship the Lord.
> **All glory to his name.**

Glory be to the Father, to the Son and to the Holy Spirit.
> **As it was in the beginning, is now and ever shall be, world without end.**

> **O Lord, forgive what we have been**
> **sanctify what we are**
> **and order what we shall be.**
> **Grant that we may always, everywhere and only do your will.**
> **Amen.**

Scripture reading, from a lectionary as appropriate.

Prayer for individual members of the wider family. Each day, members in different geographical regions may be prayed for by name.

The Teulu Trefeca Prayer. Groups may wish to replace the first paragraph with their own community prayer.

Lord God, we praise you
that from a family that lived in Trefeca
you raised up and sent out your servant Howell Harris
to renew your Church in our land.
We thank you, too, for his vision in gathering back in Trefeca
a community who worked and lived and worshipped together.
> **May we, as members of the Trefeca family today,**
> **continue to gather together and to be sent out by you.**

Gathered from our different traditions, ages,

languages and backgrounds,
we celebrate our unity in Jesus Christ your Son.
Sent out with our different gifts
and different opportunities for service,
we celebrate the power of your Holy Spirit,
still at work in our land.

Gathered to listen and to learn,
we commit ourselves to discovering
the new work you have for us today.
Sent out with a wider vision of the task,
we commit ourselves and our churches to costly discipleship.

Gathered in our weakness and emptiness,
we need to receive from your fullness.
Sent out in your strength
we thank you for what you will do in us and through us.

We hold before you, Lord,
each member of the staff,
and those who will visit, or stay in, Trefeca [*or* our community] today.

Any particular events or people are named as appropriate.

In each one and through each one
may your will be done,
in Jesus' name. Amen.

Prayers of intercession. These may include a monthly cycle of intercessions. For example:

We pray …

for those who live under the shadow of war, in constant fear, anxiety and dread, that they may be able to keep hold of hope and not be overwhelmed by hatred and the urge for revenge.

for the farmers of our country, that they may be able to continue through all difficulties and develop an industry that will be able to feed us and provide a living for rural families, while taking care of the earth that was given to us by God.

for those who meet to worship Sunday by Sunday, that they may give themselves to worship with true hearts and love towards our Lord.

**O Lord of love and peace, move in our hearts and in the hearts of
all people, that injustice and strife may be ended everywhere. Set
up your kingdom of peace in our hearts, in our homes, in our communities, in our nations and throughout the whole world. Amen.**

From Coleg Trefeca

Gweddi ar gyfer y Teulu

Gellir cyd-adrodd y llinellau mewn print tywyll.

Arglwydd agor ein gwefusau
a'n genau a fynegant dy foliant.
Addolwn yr Arglwydd
Gogoniant i'w enw.
Gogoniant i'r Tad, y Mab a'r Ysbryd Glân.
**Fel yr oedd yn y dechrau, y mae yr awr hon ac y bydd yn wastad,
yn oes oesoedd.**

**O Arglwydd, maddau i ni yr hyn a fuom
sancteiddia yr hyn ydym
bendithia yr hyn a fyddwn
Boed i ni gyflawni dy ewyllys di yn unig bob amser ac ymhob man.
Amen.**

Darlleniadau o'r Ysgrythur, o ddarlleniadur sy'n addas.

*Gweddi dros aelodau unigol y teulu. Bob dydd, gellir gweddïo dros aelodau
mewn gwahanol ardaloedd yn ôl eu henwau.*
*Gweddi Teulu Trefeca. Gall grwpiau osod eu gweddi gymunedol eu hunain yn
lle'r paragraff cyntaf.*

Arglwydd Dduw, rydym yn dy glodfori
i ti godi o blith teulu yn Nhrefeca
dy was Howell Harris, a'i ddanfon allan
i adnewyddu'r eglwys yn ein gwlad.
Diolchwn i ti hefyd am ei weledigaeth
pan fu'n casglu ynghyd yn Nhrefeca
gymuned i gyd-weithio, cyd-fyw a chyd-addoli.
**Boed i ni, aelodau o deulu Trefeca heddiw,
barhau i ddod ynghyd, a chael ein danfon allan gennyt ti.**

Wedi dod ynghyd o blith sawl traddodiad, cenhedlaeth,
iaith a chefndir,
fe ddathlwn ein hundod yn Iesu Grist dy Fab.
Wedi'n danfon allan gyda'n hamrywiol ddoniau
at amrywiol gyfleoedd i wasanaethu,
fe ddathlwn rym dy Ysbryd Glân
sydd o hyd ar waith yn ein gwlad.

Wedi dod ynghyd i wrando, ac i ddysgu –
fe ymrwymwn i ddarganfod y gwaith newydd
sydd gennyt ar ein cyfer heddiw.
Wedi'n danfon allan gyda gweledigaeth lawnach o'r gwaith
fe ymrwymwn ein hunain a'n heglwysi i ddisgyblaeth gostus.

Wedi dod ynghyd yn wan ac yn wag,
mae arnom angen dy lawnder di.
Wedi'n danfon allan yn dy nerth
fe ddiolchwn i ti am bob dim a wnei di ynom ni a thrwom ni.

Fe ddaliwn o'th flaen, Arglwydd
bob aelod o'r staff,
a phawb a fydd yn ymweld â Threfeca heddiw

[gan enwi yma yn ôl y gofyn unrhyw ddigwyddiadau neu bobl neilltuol].

Ymhob un, a thrwy bob un,
gwneler dy ewyllys di,
yn enw Iesu. Amen.

Gweddïau Eiriolaeth, yn cynnwys cynllun misol eiriolaeth e.e.

Gweddïwn …
dros rai sydd yn byw yng nghysgod rhyfel, mewn ofn a phryder a dychryn
dibaid, ar iddynt allu cadw gafael ar obaith a pheidio â chael eu llethu gan
gasineb â'r awydd i ddial.

dros amaethwyr ein gwlad, ar iddynt allu dal ati trwy bob anhawster a
datblygu diwydiant fydd yn gallu ein bwydo a darparu bywoliaeth i
deuluoedd cefn gwlad, gan ofalu am y ddaear a roddwyd i ni gan Dduw.

dros bawb sy'n cyfarfod o Sul i Sul i addoli Duw, iddynt ymroi i addoli gyda
chalon gywir a chariad tuag at ein Harglwydd.

O Arglwydd cariad a heddwch, cyffwrdd ein calonnau ni a chalonnau pawb oll, fel y ceir diwedd ar anghyfiawnder ac ymrafael ymhob man. Boed i heddwch deyrnasu yn ein calonnau, yn ein cartrefi, yn ein cymunedau, yn ein cenhedloedd a thrwy'r byd i gyd. Amen.

gan Goleg Trefeca

A reflection on the parable of the sower

This form of Morning Prayer is especially suitable for use in the context of a parish mission.

To create a visual display, newspaper may be spread out, with leaves and gravel scattered on one part, rocks and stones on another, weeds on a third, and then rich soil. Smaller displays can also be prepared and given to those participating, so that each can touch them and use them for meditation during the various stages of the reflection.

Opening reading: Isaiah 6:1–9

Leader   God who is holy invites us to come into his presence. Let us spend a moment recognising his call, and, like Isaiah, respond: 'Here I am, Lord, send me.'

A song may follow, such as 'Let all that is within me cry holy'.

Leader   Let us spend some time reflecting on the greatness of God. How have we experienced his holiness?

Participants are now invited to pray out loud, mentioning things for which they can praise God. The leader then draws people's attention to the display and invites them to meditate on how this awesome God entered our world with all its frailties and limitations. The newspaper is a reminder that God is interested in our human stories, and became involved in them. He taught us about the extraordinary by using the ordinary: rocks, stones, plants, soil. People spend a moment reflecting on this truth and its implications.

Second reading: Luke 8:4–8

Leader   Let us now take each section of the parable and prayerfully examine it.

Reader   The ones on the path are those who have heard; then the devil comes and takes away the words from their hearts, so that they may not believe and be saved.

Leader   In what ways am I careless with the grace that I have been given? How do I let the devil rob me of God's word; or how are others robbed?

Let us spend a moment praying for those who have heard about Jesus but, for different reasons, have not responded, maybe through a lack of credible witness from the Church or individual Christians, or because they do not feel welcome, or believe that they could not belong to a church. Let us allow God to place situations or people on our hearts.

A short time of silence.

Reader   The ones on the rock are those who, when they hear the word, receive it with joy. But these have no root; they believe only for a while, and in a time of testing drop away.

Leader   What things block me, stop me growing, putting down roots? Is it fear? Apathy? Doubt? Are there particular experiences or people that block me? Choose one of these blocks and decide to hand it over to Jesus.

Let us also take a moment to pray for people who experience blocks in knowing Christ, be it from their past or present situations. Let us ask the Lord to remove these blocks, that they may go deeper into his truth and his love.

A short time of silence.

Reader   As for what fell among the thorns, these are the ones who hear; but as they go on their way, they are choked by the cares and riches and pleasures of life, and their fruit does not mature.

Leader   What entraps me, holds me in bondage, preventing me from becoming free? Are there attitudes or habits of which I need to repent? Let us take a moment to seek the Lord's forgiveness.

Let us also remember those in leadership, praying that they may have integrity of heart, honesty and uprightness.

A short time of silence.

Reader   But as for that in the good soil, these are the ones who, when they hear the word, hold it fast in an honest and good heart, and bear fruit with patient endurance.

Leader   To bear fruit for God's kingdom demands perseverance. Let us pray for enduring faith, which does not give in to temptation or collapse at the first encounter with failure. Let us consider the fruit of the Spirit: love, joy, peace, patience, kindness, goodness, faithfulness, humility, self-control. Which quality will I especially ask for today?

A final time of silence.

Leader   He can use our lives. Amen.

From the Sion Community for Evangelism

Morning worship

This liturgy is suitable for Friday or the passion season.

Leader   In the name of the searching Father;
In the name of the servant Son;
In the name of the purging Spirit;
In Love's name, the Three-in-One.

All   **Amen.**

Leader   On this day [*or* at this time] of the Saviour's passion, let us be one with him in his wounds.

Leader   We seek to tread in the steps of Christ.
All   **In the steps of Christ, our Champion and King.**

Leader   He has shown us the way when strong, when weak.
All   **He is our master in everything.**

Psalm 22:1–19 may be read, or key verses from the psalm of the day.

After each of the following laments there is a pause.

Leader	May I weep for pride and loose talk …
	May I weep for the blame heaped on others …
	May I weep for things I clutch at …
All	**Strip from me, O God:**
	Pretence and divided loyalties;
	Grudges and compulsive habits;
	Lustful alighting places;
	Unloving relationships;
	Self-sufficient attitudes.

Leader	May we weep for our hollow society …
	May we weep for neglect and brutality …
	May we weep for blighted lives …
All	**May holy Jesus pardon us for these sins,**
	Free us from these evils,
	And power us into new ways.

Reader	Let us attend, the Word of God comes to us.
All	**Thanks be to God.**

Reader	Illumine our hearts, O Lord, implant in us a desire for your truth; may all that is false within us flee.

Old Testament reading.

Leader	Lord, you were born in an outhouse, an outsider.
All	**Help us to sense you in our birth.**

Leader	You were thirty years at the carpenter's bench.
All	**Help us to find you in our work.**

Leader	You were driven to the sands by the searching Spirit.
All	**Strip from us what is not of you.**

Leader	You were alone, without comfort or food.
All	**Help us to rely on you alone.**

Leader	You were tested by the evil one; you clung to no falsehood.
All	**Break in us the hold of power and pride.**

Leader	You knew deep tears and weakness.
All	**Help us to be vulnerable for you.**

| Leader | You followed to the end the way of the cross. |
| All | **Help us to be faithful to you in all our ways.** |

New Testament reading, followed by silent meditation

| Leader | Christ of the scars, into your hands we place the broken, the wounded, the hungry and the homeless … |

Christ of the scars, into your hands we place those who have been bereaved or betrayed; those who have suffered loss of health or esteem, family or friends, employment or home …

Christ of the scars, into your hands we place unwanted babies, children abused, neighbours defamed, lovers spurned, spouses deserted …

Christ of the scars, into your hands we place those who are victims of violence or vandalism, false accusation or sharp practice …

The Lord's Prayer, free prayer or a time of silent waiting may follow.

| Leader | Father, in the life of Jesus you have shown us the way. |
| All | **Give us his spirit of self-discipline; lead us more deeply into the way of the cross.** |

| Leader | Before his hands were stretched out on the cross, they were stretched out in love to children, women and men. |
| All | **May your way of the cross be our way, that we too may stretch out our hands in love to all. Amen.** |

From the Bowthorpe Ecumenical Community

A workaday prayer

Father God,
We come to you from different traditions, yet each of us aware that you are our Father. We are here, seeking to serve you in our everyday lives.

We have much to share.
We have much to learn.

Help us, not just to hear, but to listen to the ideas and inspirations of others.

By your word, and through our fellowship together, make it clear that you are the one who must daily lead us.

We shall meet many people this day.
Some will know you,
Others will be seeking you,
Many will not give you a thought.

May the way in which we live, and the things that we say, touch the lives of others with your love.

We are your children and you are our Father.
Nothing can separate us from your love.

Thank you, Lord.
Amen.
>   *From the Daily Bread Co-operative*

Midday Prayer

This is said or sung all together.
✠ *indicates that you may make the sign of the cross.*

✠ In the name of the Father,
and of the Son,
and of the Holy Spirit. Amen.

Opening Sentences
Let the beauty of the Lord our God be upon us.
Establish thou the work of our hands;
establish thou the work of our hands.

The Lord's Prayer
Our Father, who art in heaven,
hallowed be thy name;
Thy kingdom come;
Thy will be done,
On earth as it is in heaven.
Give us this day our daily bread
and forgive us our trespasses
as we forgive those who trespass against us.
And lead us not into temptation;
but deliver us from evil. Amen.

Declaration of faith
We believe and trust in God the Father Almighty.
We believe and trust in Jesus Christ his Son.
We believe and trust in the Holy Spirit.
We believe and trust in the Three in One.

Canticle
Teach us, dear Lord, to number our days,
        that we may apply our hearts unto wisdom.
Oh, satisfy us early with thy mercy,
that we may rejoice and be glad all of our days.
And let the beauty of the Lord our God be upon us;
and establish thou the work of our hands.

And let the beauty of the Lord our God be upon us;
and establish thou the work of our hands, dear Lord.

Blessing
Let nothing disturb thee,
nothing affright thee;
all things are passing,
God never changeth.
Patient endurance attaineth to all things;
who God possesseth
in nothing is wanting;
alone God sufficeth.

✠ In the name of the Father,
and of the Son,
and of the Holy Spirit. Amen.
From the Northumbria Community

An alternative Midday Prayer

I bow before your Presence,
You who are common to us all.

*Rhythmic breathing of the name 'Jesus'. As you breathe out the last syllable 'us',
let tensions, hurts or failures flow out like an ebbing tide. As you breathe in the
first syllable 'Je', desire to be filled with the fullness and goodness of God.*

Fill me with the Deep Wisdom.
Fill me with the Great Compassion.
Fill me with the Serene Peace.

Pause.

Let forgiveness flow.
Let love come forth.
Let energy return.

Pause.

Deep peace of the quiet earth.
Deep peace of the flowing air.
Deep peace of the floating spheres.

Deep peace of the Son of peace.

Silent communion with the source of all.
A Bible verse may be read.

Kindle in us the fire of love.
Bring us alive.
Give warmth to our work.

Dear Jesus, at this hour you hung on the Cross, stretching out your arms in love to all. May all the peoples of the world be drawn to your love, especially the people I shall work with next.

Realising that we are all nourished from the same source, may we so live that others are not deprived of food or friends, of shelter or smiles, of pure air or good earth, or of the desire to live fully human lives.

Take time to visualise this prayer:

Your kingdom come.
Your will be done,
On earth as it is in heaven.

The eternal Creator keep us.
The beloved Companion beside us.
The Spirit's smile upon us.
From the Community of Aidan and Hilda

We are here

The words in bold may be said all together.

We are here, God.
We have felt your touch in the sunlight
seen your power in the salt waves.
We have wondered at your mystery in the stars
and we marvel that the maker of the universe
knows us by name.
We are here, God.
    We are here to praise and worship you.

We are here, Jesus.

We know that you came to find us.
We have listened to your words
and smiled at your stories.
We have felt the warmth of your love, and
we thank you that you have called us friends.
We are here, Jesus.
> **We are here to praise and worship you.**

We are here, Holy Spirit.
We are grateful for your presence
grateful for the way you bring us close –
for the way you comfort us and challenge us
and keep us right.
We are here, Holy Spirit.
> **We are here to praise and worship you.**

We are here, God,
in this moment, in this place
and we thank you that you are here with us.
You know us, God.
We do not have to pretend with you.
In the silence of your love, we bring you
the things that trouble us
that harm us
that make us feel ashamed or afraid.

Silence.

God, have mercy on us.
> **Christ, have mercy on us.**
God, have mercy on us.

Silence.

Listen to the words of Jesus,
words that we can trust:
'Don't be afraid
Your sins are forgiven
I love you
Come and follow me.'
Thanks be to God.
> **Amen.**
> *From the Iona Community*

Evening Prayer

Leader   Spirit of the Risen Christ,
As the lamps light up the evening,
Shine into our hearts
And kindle in us the fire of your love.

Candles may be lit.
These words may be said or sung:

Leader   The light of Christ has come into the world.
All   **The light of Christ has come into the world.**

Leader   Let us give thanks always and for everything
To the Lord our God.
He led our ancestors in the faith
By a pillar of cloud by day
And a pillar of fire by night,
And prepared a lamp for his anointed.
All   **The light of Christ has come into the world.**

A hymn may be sung.

All   **O Lord Jesus Christ, light of the world,**
By your cross you have overcome
All darkness that oppresses.
Come and shine on us here in ...
That we may grow and live together in your love
Which makes us one with all humanity. Amen.

A psalm may be read.
This may be followed by a brief silence.

Leader   We offer you, Lord,
The troubles of this day.
We lay down our burdens at your feet.
Forgive us our sins,
Give us your peace,
And help us to receive your word.

All   **In the name of Christ, Amen.**

There may be a reading from the Bible.

Reader   Let us attend. Hear the Word of God in …

           at close:

Reader   This is the Word of the Lord.
All   **Thanks be to God.**

Silent reflection on the Word.

Leader   Let us give thanks to God, our Father
           Always and in everything.
           Let us thank him for this day's gifts
           Of life, friendship and creation,
           And recall the blessings of this day.

Intercessions.
There may be a said or sung response such as the following:

All   **May our prayers rise like incense**
           And our hands like an evening offering.

Leader   Into your hands, O Lord,
           We place all whom we have met this day;
           And our families, our neighbours,
           And our brothers and sisters in Christ.
           Enfold them in your will.

Response.

Leader   Into your hands, O Lord,
           We place all who are victims of prejudice,
           Oppression or neglect,
           Especially the frail and unwanted.
           May everyone be cherished
           From conception to the grave.

Response.

Leader   Into your hands, O Lord,
We commit all who are restless, sick,
Or prey to the powers of evil.
Keep guard over them.

Response.

Free prayer.

Leader   Lighten our darkness, Lord, we pray,
And in your great mercy defend us
From all dangers and perils of this night,
For the love of your only Son,
Our Saviour, Jesus Christ. Amen.

From the Bowthorpe Ecumenical Community

Night Prayer

Leader   In the name of the restful Father,
        In the name of the calming Son,
        In the name of the peaceful Spirit.
        May we and God be one.

Leader   I place my soul and body
        Under your guarding this night, O God,
        O Father of help to frail pilgrims,
        Protector of heaven and earth.

All   **I place my soul and body**
        Under your guiding this night, O Christ,
        O Son of the tears and the piercings,
        May your cross this night be my shield.

Leader   I place my soul and body
        Under your glowing this night, O Spirit,
        O gentle Companion, and soul Friend,
        My heart's eternal Warmth.

Say or sing Psalm 134:

Come bless the Lord, all you servants of the Lord,
Who stand by night in the house of the Lord;
Lift up your hands in the holy place,
Come bless the Lord, come bless the Lord.

Leader   May that part of me which did not grow at morning
        Grow at nightfall …

There may be a brief pause.

Leader   You are our Saviour and Lord.
All   **In our stumbling be our Shield.**

Leader   In our tiredness be our Rest.
All   **In our darkness be our Light.**

Reader	O Christ, Son of the living God,
	May your holy angels guard our sleep;
	May they watch over us as we rest
	And hover around our beds.

Let them reveal to us in our dreams
Visions of your glorious truth.
May no fears or worries delay
Our willing, prompt repose.

These or other words of Christ may be said:

Come to me, all you who are weary and burdened, and I will give you rest. Take my yoke upon you and learn from me, for I am gentle and humble of heart, and you will find rest for your souls.

This may be followed by silence, during which other words from God may be spoken spontaneously.

Leader My dear ones bless, O God, and keep in every place where they are, especially …

Dear ones may be named.

All **May the great and strong heavenly army**
Encircle us all with their outstretched arms,
To protect us from the hostile powers,
To put balm into our dreams,
To give us contented, sweet repose.

Leader I lie down this night with God,
All **And God will lie down with me;**

Leader I lie down this night with Christ,
All **And Christ will lie down with me;**

Leader I lie down this night with the Spirit,
All **And the Spirit will lie down with me;**

Leader God and Christ and the Spirit,
All **Lying down with me.**

I make the sign of the Cross of Christ,
My Christ, my Shield, my Encircler;
Each day, each night, in light, in dark,
My Treasure, my dear One.

The almighty and merciful Three encircle us,
that awake we may watch with Christ,
and asleep we may rest in peace.

From the Community of Aidan and Hilda

Anthem to the Virgin Mary

We greet you, holy Queen,
our life, our joy and hope.
Mother full of mercy, we cry to you in trust.
Exiled children of fallen Eve,
see our sighs and tears,
see our world of sadness,
Mother, plead for us.
Turn then towards us those eyes that plead our cause,
and when our life on earth is done,
show us then your Son,
blessed fruit of your virgin womb,
Jesus Christ our God.
O Mary, full of kindness,
O Mary, full of love,
O joyful Mary, full of peace and grace.

From the Ecumenical Society of the Blessed Virgin Mary

Night blessing

May the Lord in heaven
Bless you tonight,
May he keep you safe,
Lead you through the night,
Sheltered from harm,
Shielded in light,
Safe in his arms tonight.

May he send his angels
To guard you in peace.

May the love of Jesus
Bless you as you sleep,
With rest deep and soft,
And dreams pure and true,
Oh Lord, hear my prayer for you.

From the Pilgrims Community

Saints

Mary

Hymn to the Virgin Mary

O Mary, little Mary,
You are the gentle breeze of Elijah,
The breath of the Spirit of God.
O Mary, little Mary,
You are the burning bush of Moses,
Which bears the Lord without being consumed.
You are 'that place near me'
Which the Lord showed to Moses.
You are the cleft in the rock
Which God covers with his hand,
While his glory passes by.

O Mary, little Mary,
Child of Jerusalem,
Mother of all nations,
Virgin of Nazareth,
You are the cloud that protects Israel,
The tent where we meet,
The Ark of the Covenant,
The place where the Lord dwells,
The sanctuary of his Shekinah.

Let the Lord come with us
If we have found favour in his eyes.
It is true that we are sinners,
But pray for us and we shall be his heritage.

From the Neocatechumenal Way

Prayer to Our Lady of Guadalupe

Dear Mother, we love you.
We thank you for your promise to help us in our need.
Teach us to find our peace in your Son, Jesus,
And bless us every day of our lives.

Help us to build a shrine in our hearts.
Make it as beautiful as the one built for you
On the Mount of Tepeyac:
A shrine full of trust, hope and love of Jesus growing stronger each day.

Mary, you have chosen to remain with us
By giving us your most wonderful and holy self-image
On Juan Diego's cloak.
May we feel your loving presence
As we look upon your face.
Like Juan, give us the courage
To bring your message of hope to everyone.

You are our Mother and our inspiration.
Hear our prayers and answer us.
Amen.

From the Franciscan Friars of the Renewal

Mary the dawn

Mary the dawn, but Christ the perfect day.
Mary the gate, but Christ the heavenly way.
Mary the root, but Christ the mystic vine.
Mary the grape, but Christ the sacred wine.
Mary the corn-sheaf, Christ the living bread.
Mary the rose-tree, Christ the rose blood-red.
Mary the fount, but Christ the cleansing flood.
Mary the chalice, Christ the saving blood.
Mary the beacon, Christ the haven's rest.
Mary the mirror, Christ the vision blest.

From the Ecumenical Society of the Blessed Virgin Mary

An act of consecration to Our Blessed Lady

O Virgin Mary, we come with confidence to you, our Mother. As preachers we take refuge with you, for you believed in the words sent from heaven and kept them in your heart.

In you was the Word made flesh, the Word we receive and contemplate, the Word we praise and preach, and by which we live. And today it is under your protection that we devote ourselves afresh to the service of the Word Incarnate.

We dedicate ourselves also to you, so that with you we may hear the Word within and, anointed by the Spirit, whose glorious shrine you are, we may be consecrated to preach the Gospel and the name of Jesus Christ, to perceive his presence in the history of our time, and so come at last to contemplate him face to face.

Through you the Father sent his Son into the world to save it. Through you may we be enabled to bear witness to that truth which sets us free, to that love which makes us one. Amen.

From the Dominican Sisters of St Joseph

The overshadowing

O Holy Spirit, Lord and giver of life, as you overshadowed Mary that she might be the Mother of Jesus our Saviour, so work silently in my heart, to form within me the fulness of his redeemed and redeeming humanity. Give me his loving heart, to burn with love for God and love for my neighbour; give me a share of his joy and sorrow, his weakness and his strength, his labour for the world's salvation. May Mary, blessed among women, Mother of our Saviour, pray for me, that Christ may be formed in me, that I may live in union of heart and will with Jesus Christ, her Son, our Lord and Saviour. Amen.

From the Ecumenical Society of the Blessed Virgin Mary

Our Mother of Good Counsel

Mary, our Mother, we thank you that we can always call upon you to help us
    in our need.
You were chosen from the whole human race and entrusted by God, Creator
    of the universe, to nurture his Son, Jesus, and to guide his steps.
It is with confidence that we come to you now and, pondering on how you
    held Jesus in your heart and in your arms,
we ask you to hold us in the same way,
so that we can be close to you and to your Son.
Show us how to reveal Jesus to others with gentleness and love, and guide us
    with wisdom and good counsel on our journey through life. Amen.

From the Clare Priory Community

Mary, servant of the Lord

Today we choose you, Mary, standing before all the saints,
To be our mother and our queen.

We dedicate ourselves to you, in humility and love;
Our bodies and our souls, our gifts and our possessions,
The merit of good deeds, those present, past and still to come.

We freely give you the right to deal with us
And everything we have, as you see fit,
For the greater glory of God, both now and in eternity.

Mary, servant of the Lord,
You gave birth to him who made us all;
Mary, mother of our God,
Blessed virgin, hear our prayer.

From the Emmanuel Community

A prayer to Mary

Oh, help me, Mary.
Be a Mother to me.
Pray for me,
Stay by me,
Help me to see
Your Son, Jesus
Among us,
Within us,
For he is our Way,
The Truth
And the Life
Of our life.
Amen.

From the Pilgrims Community

Aidan

The mantle

This liturgy is especially suitable for the Feast of St Aidan, 31 August.

Leader In the name of the sending Father;
In the name of the gentle Son;
In the name of the teaching Spirit;
In Love's name, the Three-in-One.

God said: 'My teaching will fall like gentle rain on tender grass.'
(Deuteronomy 32:2)

Lord, whose gentle apostle Aidan befriended everyone he met
with Jesus Christ; give us his humble, Spirit-filled zeal, that we
may inspire others to learn your ways, and to pass on the torch
of faith.

All **All that I am, all that I do, all whom I'll meet today I offer now
to you.**

There may be singing.

Leader Ebb tide, full tide, praise the Lord of land and sea.
All **Barren rocks, darting birds, praise his holy name!**

Leader Poor folk, ruling folk, praise the Lord of land and sea.
All **Pilgrimed sands, sea-shelled strands, praise his holy name!**

Leader Fierce lions, gentle lambs, praise the Lord of land and sea.
All **Noble women, mission priests, praise his holy name!**

Leader Chanting children, slaves set free, praise the Lord of land and
sea.
All **Old and young and all the land, praise his holy name!**

Reader *Psalm 103:1-18*
This response may be used after verses 5,10,14,18:

All	**Do not forget how kind he is.**

Alleluias may be sung.

Reader	*Isaiah 6:1-8*

Reader	O Aidan, you had a vision of a population transformed in Christ.
	You had the faith to come.
	You had the gentleness to win the hearts of king and commoner.
	You ministered in power and patience to the sick and dying.
	You created teamwork.
	Your visits to tell people Good News gave your team a pattern to follow.
	You loved the people of the island.
	You lived simply and prayed much.
	You prepared a mission to the kingdom.
	You influenced many to reach others for Christ.
	You are Christ to the nation.
	You are apostle to this land.
	You are in pain that people here are heedless of your Lord.
	You will not rest till they are won.

Leader	Father, put the mantle of Aidan on us.

Song: 'I, the Lord of sea of sky'

Reader	*Matthew 11:25-30*

This may be followed by silence, teaching or sharing.

Leader	Lord, Aidan was humble and loving; forgive us for being proud.
	Lord, have mercy.
All	**Lord, have mercy.**
Leader	Lord, Aidan was a faithful shepherd; forgive us for being faithless.
	Christ, have mercy.
All	**Christ, have mercy.**
Leader	Lord, Aidan brought the torch of Christ for all to see; forgive us for hiding the light.

Lord, have mercy.

All   **Lord, have mercy.**

Leader   Lord, we of this day are children of confusion;
Restore the vision of God to us.
The noise of the city deafens us to the still, small voice;
Restore the hearing of God to us.
The pace of modern living chokes us;
Restore the alertness of God to us.
The pride of modern living imprisons us;
Restore the liberty of God to us.

We pray for the Holy Island of Lindisfarne:
Here be the peace of those who do your will;
Here be the peace of brother serving other;
Here be the peace of holy ones obeying;
Here be the peace of praise by dark and day.

Reader   Set us free, O God, to cross barriers for you,
As you crossed barriers for us.
Spirit of God, make us open to others in listening,
Generous to others in giving,
And sensitive to others in praying,
Through Jesus Christ our Lord.

We pray for the conversion of the English people.
We pray for the renewal of the English Church.

We pray that you will raise up new communities of witness.
We pray for this church ... *(free prayer)*

There may be singing.

Leader   From today and always may we:
Look upon each person we meet with the eyes of Christ;
Speak to each person we meet with the words of Christ;
And go wherever we are led with the peace of Christ.
Amen.

From the Community of Aidan and Hilda

Caedmon

A call to be good news to the poor

Caedmon of Whitby (?–608) loved to listen. Music thrilled him, and other people's stories, songs and ballads carried him along as helplessly as a small boat on a rising tide. But he couldn't play a note on the harp. Nor could he sing a note in tune. If he tried to join in with a song when he was a child everyone else was unable to keep singing. Besides, he could never remember any words. He couldn't even tell a joke and get it right. His head got all confused, and the words tumbled out back to front.

So a night like tonight was torture for him. Heaven and hell, that's what it was. To hear each person share a song, to listen to the music of the harp as it was passed along, strummed by one, touched gently by another – nothing could be sweeter. But the nearer it came to Caedmon's turn the more a sickness rose from his stomach, and his bowels stirred uneasily. At the last possible moment he could he would run out of the hall.

Once outside he went straight to the cattle shed to check on his beasts, then threw himself down on his bed, and passed into a fitful sleep.

In his dream a man stood before him. 'Sing for me, Caedmon,' he said. 'Sing for me.'

'I can't sing,' Caedmon protested. 'Why do you think I'm out here in the cattle shed, instead of inside at the feast?'

'Sing anyway, sing for me.'

'I don't know what to sing.'

'Sing about the beginning of the world, and sing about creation.'

So Caedmon sang a song of praise to the Guardian of heaven, the Father of glory. And in his dream he was able to sing . . . a song so beautiful it could make you cry.

When he awoke, the song was still with him, and he sang it for God and for himself. He sang it for the steward of all the farmlands of the abbey. He sang it for Abbess Hild herself when the steward told her what had happened. He sang it for all the scholars and holy men and women of the abbey the Lady Hild had called for. He sang it for the people of Whitby and everyone in the countryside round about.

Now someone else looked after the cattle, while whoever could read aloud spoke aloud the Scriptures and translated them for Caedmon. Each night he sang aloud the things he had heard until a new song was prepared, explaining the Bible to his people in their own language. And now for all his life his mouth spoke out the truths that filled his heart.

This form of prayer may be used:

- *on Caedmon's day (11 February);*
- *on pilgrimage to Whitby;*
- *by any storyteller, singer or songwriter;*
- *by those concerned to be a voice for those who have no voice;*
- *for those committed to solidarity with the poor and disadvantaged.*

All who wish may read in turn.
* Indicates a change of reader.
With a large group, split into two halves and read alternately.

*   I cannot speak,
     unless you loose my tongue;
     I only stammer,
     and I speak uncertainly;
     but if you touch my mouth,
     my Lord,
     then I will sing the story
     of your wonders!

*   Teach me to hear that story,
     through each person,
     to cradle a sense of wonder
     in their life,
     to honour the hard-earned wisdom
     of their sufferings,
     to waken their joy
     that the King of all kings
     stoops down
     to wash their feet,
     and looking up
     into their face
     says,
     'I know – I understand.'

*   This world has become
     a world of broken dreams
     where dreamers are hard to find
     and friends are few.

*   Lord, be the gatherer of our dreams.
      You set the countless stars in place,
      and found room for each of them to shine.
      You listen for us in your heaven-bright hall.
      Open our mouths to tell our tales of wonder.

*   Teach us again the greatest story ever:
      the One who made the worlds
      became a little, helpless child,
      then grew to be a carpenter
      with deep, far-seeing eyes.

*   In time, the carpenter began to travel,
      in every village challenging the people
      to leave behind their selfish ways,
      be washed in living water,
      and let God be their King.

*   The ordinary people crowded round him,
      frightened to miss
      a word that he was speaking,
      bringing their friends, their children,
      all the sick and tired,
      so everyone could meet him,
      everyone be touched and given life.

*   Some religious people were embarrassed
      – they did not like the company he kept,
      and never knew just what he would do next.

*   He said:
      'How dare you wrap God up
      in good behaviour,
      and tell the poor that they
      should be like you?
      How can you live at ease
      with riches and success,
      while those I love go hungry
      and are oppressed?
      It really is for such a time as this
      that I was given breath.'

*   His words were dangerous,
    not safe or tidy.

*   In secret his opponents said:
    'It surely would be better that
    one person die.'
    'I think that would be better,
    if he could.'
    Expediency would be the very death of him.
    He died because *they* thought it might be good.

*   You died that we might be forgiven, Lord;
    but that was not the end.
    You plundered death,
    and made its jail-house shudder
    – strode into life
    to meet your startled friends.

*   I have a dream
    that all the world will meet you,
    and know you, Jesus,
    in your living power,
    that someday soon
    all people everywhere will hear your story,
    and hear it in a way they understand.

Each may say (or the leader may say and all repeat together):

    I cannot speak,
    unless you loose my tongue;
    I only stammer,
    and I speak uncertainly;
    but if you touch my mouth,
    my Lord,
    then I will sing the story
    of your wonders!

*   So many who have heard
    forget to tell the story.

All say together:

**Here am I, my Jesus:
teach me.**

From the Northumbria Community

Francis

O Blessed Poet

Holy Father Francis,
the world is still impoverished
by its feverish desire to amass riches,
but you call us to enrich it
with the Holy Poverty of Christ.

This age grows colder
because of its selfish, unchannelled, heated passion,
while you call us
to bring blessed, refreshing coolness
through unselfish, seraphic love.

O Blessed Poet of God,
pray that we too may call down Christ's mercy
upon this beautiful but broken earth.
Amen.
> *From the Franciscan Friars of the Renewal*

Prayer to St Francis

O St Francis, stigmatised on La Verna,
the world longs for you,
that icon of the crucified Jesus.
It has need of your heart,
open to God and others;
of your bare, wounded feet,
of your pierced hands raised in supplication.
It longs for your voice so frail,
yet forceful with the power of the Gospel.
Francis, help the people of this age
to recognise the evil of sin
and to seek purification from it in penance.
Help them to become free from the very structures of sin
that oppress today's society.

Rekindle in the consciousness of those in government
an urgent need for peace between nations and peoples.
Instil in young people your freshness of life
that is capable of withstanding the snares
of the many cultures of death.
To those injured by every type of evil
teach, O Francis, the joy of being able to forgive.
To all those crucified by suffering, hunger and war,
reopen the doors of hope.
Help us!
You who brought Christ so close to your age,
help us to bring Christ close to our age,
to our difficult and critical times.

From the Franciscan Friars of the Renewal

Testament Prayer of St Francis

We adore you, most holy Lord Jesus Christ,
Here, and in all your churches throughout the world,
And we bless you,
Because by your holy Cross you have redeemed the world.

From the Franciscan Friars of the Renewal

Celebrations

Baptism

Water

In my heat
of anguish
and fear
I am refreshed
by the sprinkling
of your
cool, refreshing
water.
In my filth
and dirtiness
I am washed
by your
pure and cleansing
water.
In my weariness
and
directionless life
I am swept along
by the strong current
of your
water.
In my half-heartedness
half-giving
half-loving
half-living
help me
to be immersed
fully
in your water
and cross
Jordan
to the
promised land.

From the Maranatha Community

The Eucharist

You are joy

O Beloved, the Eucharist is the Sacrament of joy. How could it be otherwise, even in difficulties? For if I possess you in the Eucharist, I enjoy your real presence and its sweetness. You alone are food and drink and the only joy in this world. You are joy. Your service is one of joy.

O Jesus, if only people knew what delights are in your service, they would all become your servants, your friends, your brothers and sisters.

O Jesus, indeed my soul is filled with the joy of your service. I love you. Today I offer you all my actions for love – only for love. Teach me to see, Beloved. Teach me to understand that love alone can be my motive in your service. Beloved of my heart, Infinite Joy, let me be your humble servant.

From the Madonna House Community

His Mass and ours

If you suffer and your suffering is such
that it prevents any activity,
remember the Mass.
Jesus in the Mass,
today as once before,
does not work, does not preach;
Jesus sacrifices himself out of love.
In life
we can do many things, say many words,
but the voice of suffering,
maybe unheard and unknown to others,
is the most powerful word,
the one that pierces heaven.
If you suffer,
immerse your pain in his;
say your Mass;
and if the world does not understand
do not worry;

all that matters
is that you are understood by Jesus, Mary, the saints.
Live with them,
and let your blood flow
for the good of humanity –
like him!
The Mass!
It is too great to understand!
His Mass, our Mass.

From the Focolare Movement

The holy things of God

This can be sung to the melody of the Gaelic carol 'Talodh Chriosda'.
'Alleluia' is pronounced in the Orthodox way: 'Al-le-e-lu-i-a'.

The holy things of God are here,
Blest and broken, quenching fear;
God's holy people, gather near,
Made one with tears of love.

Alleluia, alleluia,
Alleluia, holy, holy Lord.

If we but knew the gift he brings,
How he longs to gather in,
And share with us the living spring
Cascading to our hearts.

In Christ there is no east or west,
One the host, and one the guests
Whom Jesus kneads with holiness;
Made one in heart and love.

From L'Arche Edinburgh

Blessings

A house blessing

Lord Jesus Christ,
who served in a home at Nazareth,
bless this house.
Drive from it all that is unworthy.

May its doors be open to those in need,
and its rooms have the light of purity.
May its walls echo gladness,
and joy shine from its windows.
May your peace protect it,
and your presence never leave it.

Help all who live here
to see ourselves as we really are,
and to care for others without self-interest.
Here may we learn to forgive,
and to bring the best out of one another.
In this home may true and tested love grow strong.
From it may we go renewed to serve our community.

From the Bowthorpe Ecumenical Community

A blessing at the doorway

May God give his blessing to the house that is here.
God bless this house from roof to floor,
from wall to wall,
from end to end,
from its foundation and in its covering.

In the strong name of the Triune God
all evil be banished,
all disturbance cease,
captive spirits freed,

God's Spirit alone
dwell within these walls.

We call upon the Sacred Three
to save, shield and surround
this house, this home,
this day, this night
and every night.

From the Northumbria Community

A blessing in the kitchen

I would welcome the poor
and honour them.
I would welcome the sick
in the presence of angels
and ask God to bless
and embrace us all.

Seeing a stranger approach,
I would put food in the eating place,
drink in the drinking place,
music in the listening place,
and look with joy for the blessing of God,
who often comes to my home
in the blessing of a stranger.

From the Northumbria Community

A blessing on meals

Blessing of loaves, blessing of fish;
thousands are fed: a gift of God.
King of the feast, lord of this fare,
bless all we have, bless all we share.

From L'Arche Edinburgh

A blessing on visitors

God's blessing be on you as you enter this place,
in the stillness and the beauty,

in the solid, simple welcome of stones,
built on faith and vision,
hallowed by prayers and pilgrim lives.

Christ's blessing be among you as you stay in this place,
in shared laughter and common tasks,
in the meeting of minds and hearts,
in the healing touch of community.

The Spirit's blessing be with you as you go from this place,
in energy restored and vision focussed,
in the stirring of your heart, tumbling into prayer and action,
in the knowledge that you are not alone.

May the blessing of God's presence be
with you and go with you,
this day and every day. Amen.
From Coleg Trefeca

Benydd ar ymwhewir

Bendith Duw fo arnoch wrth ddod i'r lle hwn.
Yn y tywelwch a'r harddwch,
yng nghroeso cadarn, syml y cerrig
a adeiladwyd ar sail ffydd a gweledigaeth,
wedi'u sancteiddio gan weddïau a bywydau'r pererinion.

Bendith Crist fo yn eich plith wrth i chi aros yn y lle hwn.
Yn y cyd-chwerthin a'r cyd-weithio,
yng nghyd-gyfarfyddiad meddyliau a chalonnau,
yng nghyffyrddiad iachusol y gymuned.

Bendith yr Ysbryd fo gyda chi wrth i chi ymadael â'r lle hwn.
Yn yr egni a adferwyd a'r weledigaeth a eglurwyd,
yn y galon sy'n llamu, yn byrlymu'n barod i weddïo a gweithredu,
yn y sicrwydd nad ydych ar eich pen eich hunan.

Boed i fendith presenoldeb Duw fod gyda
chi a mynd gyda chi,
y diwrnod hwn a phob dydd. Amen.
gan Goleg Trefeca

A blessing on those departing

May the peace of the Lord Christ go with you,
wherever he may send you.
May he guide you through the wilderness,
protect you through the storm.
May he bring you home rejoicing
at the wonders he has shown you.
May he bring you home rejoicing
once again into our doors.

From the Northumbria Community

Community Prayers

Aidan and Hilda

Lord Jesus, simplicity and a deep love for people shone out of your apostle,
Aidan.
Grant that, like him, we may be gentle in our loving and bold in our speaking,
that we might inspire others to learn your ways,
and so pass on the fire of faith.

You made Hilda shine like a jewel in the land.
Help us, like her, to encourage others to their callings,
to reconcile those who are divided,
and to praise you with our whole being.

Grant, O Lord, that your Church in this land may be true to its birthright.
Kindle in our community the adventure of obedience,
the single eye, the humble and generous heart,
which marked Aidan, Hilda and your Celtic saints.
Amen.

From the Community of Aidan and Hilda

Because . . .

The words in bold may be said all together.

Because Jesus entirely gave up his life to give us life, we in turn, conscious of
our weakness, irreversibly

commit our lives.

Because the hunger of those starving to death has no other solution than our
sharing, because the dream of a more just and fraternal society is not enough,

starting now, today, we share our belongings.

Because our children enjoy living in community and because many other
children are poor and naked, and we want to leave as a heritage the ideal and
reality of a better world,

we choose to share our inheritances.

Because, whether consecrated in celibacy or in the bonds of marriage, we want a life in conformity to the love of God,

we count on the help of our brothers and sisters to grow in faithfulness.

Because truth is priceless, and lies are common currency; because truth makes us free,

we try to be truthful with one another.

Because the division among Christians is the greatest obstacle to evangelisation; because we believe that the prayer of Jesus Christ for unity will be granted, 'that they all may be one so that the world may believe',

together, Orthodox, Protestants, Catholics, without waiting any longer, we follow the humble path of a shared daily life.

Because we want to be available for the harvest which is abundant and because Jesus saves the world by his obedience,

we choose to live in obedience and submission to each other.

Because the power of the Holy Spirit measures up to the problems of our time and because the strength of God triumphs over our weakness,

we ask for the help of the Holy Spirit.

Because we love each other; because joy is victorious,

we commit our lives in this community to serve the Church and the unity of Christians.

From the Chemin Neuf Community

Your will and your way

We bring to your love, Lord,
The work of all at Daily Bread Co-operative;
That in constant prayer
We may learn your will and your way of doing things.

Grant that we may value the gift of life,
And use our time for your glory.

From the Daily Bread Co-operative

Prayer of the Companions of St Francis

Draw us to yourself, most worthy Father, Francis, that we may run after your fragrance of holiness. As you know, we are lukewarm because of our sloth, languid because of our idleness, half-alive because of our negligence. This little flock is following you with hesitant steps. Our weak eyes cannot bear the dazzling rays of your perfection. Renew our days as from the beginning, O mirror and model of perfection, and do not allow us, who are like you in our profession, to be unlike you in our lives.

Holy Father, remember all your sons and daughters who, surrounded by inextricable dangers, follow your footsteps though from so great a distance. Give us strength that we may resist; purify us that we may gleam forth; fill us with joy that we may be happy. Pray that the spirit of grace and of prayer may be poured upon us; that we may have the true humility you had; that we may observe the poverty you observed; that we may be filled with the charity with which you always loved Christ Crucified, who, with the Father and the Holy Spirit, lives and reigns, world without end. Amen.

From the Franciscan Friars of the Renewal

The Hengrave Prayer

Lord Jesus,
Your sign of reconciliation is the cross,
In all its breadth and length and height and depth.
Teach us to share it with you and our sisters and brothers,
So that we may learn to act justly,
To walk humbly,
And to love tenderly,
And so,
Waiting upon the Spirit,
Become instruments of your peace,
To the glory of the Father.
Amen.

From the Hengrave Community

A Heath Town creed

We believe in a God who is the Creator of everything.
We believe in a God who is a loving, heavenly Father.
We believe in a God who is a creative Spirit, within us and all around us.
We believe in a God whose ways are strange and who sometimes seems not
to be there when we need him.

We believe in a God who is black, white, male and female.
We believe in a God who is everywhere, in everyone and in everything.

We believe in a God who is good and forgives us – no matter what.
We believe in a God who is Jesus Christ, our brother, and like us in all ways that
are good.
We believe in a God who especially loves the poor and little children.
We believe in a God who is the only Way, the only Truth and the only Life.
We believe that we are made in the image of God and that we can become
like him.
I believe that I am his child.

We believe that we are all his family and that he rejects no one, no matter who
they are or what they have done.
We believe that he gives us the freedom to question who he is.
We believe that he has called each one of us for a special purpose in life.

We believe that God is with us when we suffer and when we are happy.
We believe that God has prepared a heaven for us when we die so that we
can be with God forever.
We believe that God is a Mystery who we won't fully understand until we
meet him in death.

We believe that God always answers our prayers, but often not as we would
like.
We believe that God helps us to live as Jesus taught us.
We believe in a God who lets us show our love for him by loving and caring
for others.

From the Hope Community

The open door

When you said that thing,
    about the door that you'd opened,
      staying open,
my heart dilated with love
    (if hearts can do such a thing).

Because I saw this door,
    carved with pomegranates and palm leaves,
      of warm eastern wood,
propped, permanently open.

And then I thought, 'What fool
    would wedge a door, never to be closed,
      when icy draughts might issue from the north,
    or stinking manure fly off the farm cart,
      as it goes past to the fields,
      and be trodden into the carpet?
And what if some foot-in-the-door salesman
    should con you into buying his wares?

Or what if such things should flow
    out from my heart,
    deep into yours,
as you *will* keep your door so widely open?'

As I wondered, you waited
quietly,
    patiently,
      tenderly,
until my heart could bear it no more
    and I came in
      through the open door.

From the House of the Open Door

A prayer for Iona

O God our Father, who gave to your servant Columba the gifts of courage, faith and cheerfulness, and sent people forth from Iona to carry the word of your Gospel to every creature, grant, we pray, a like spirit to your Church, even at this present time. Further in all things the purpose of our community, that hidden things may be revealed to us, and new ways found to touch the hearts of all. May we preserve with each other sincere charity and peace, and, if it be your holy will, grant that a place of your abiding be continued still to be a sanctuary and a light. Through Jesus Christ our Lord. Amen.

From the Iona Community

A place of hope

'A place of hope'
they say;
and in their thousands
they journey, year by year,
to this tiny island
on the margins of Europe.
Sunswept and windswept,
yet always deeply
a place of transformation,
a sacred place on earth:
a pilgrim's place
of light and shadow
energy and challenge.

We need you, Iona,
with your alternative vision,
with your ever-present questions
your often uncomfortable silence;
for you are a place of prayer,
of Christ's abiding;
weaving a rainbow of meaning
through the endless busyness of our days,
holding together the frayed threads
of our fleeting devotion,
opening a path for healing and for peace.
Not momentary healing
nor easy faith,
but struggle, commitment,
and an ongoing conversion
are your gifts for our
broken yet beautiful lives.

From the Iona Community

The L'Arche prayer

Father, through Jesus our Lord and our brother
We ask you to bless us.
Grant that L'Arche may be a true home
Where the poor in spirit may find life,
Where those who suffer may find hope.
Keep in your loving care
All those who come.
Spirit of God, give us greatness of heart
That we may welcome all those you send.
Make us compassionate
That we may heal and bring peace.
Help us to see, to serve and to love.
O Lord, through the hands of your little ones, bless us.
Through the eyes of those who are rejected, smile on us.
O Lord, grant freedom, fellowship and unity
To all your children,
And welcome everyone into your kingdom.
Amen.
  From L'Arche Lambeth

Gather in the gift of our lives

Gather in the gift of our lives,
blessed, broken, shared.
Reveal our hearts,
to love as you adore.

Abba, Father,
in your hands we place our spirit
and our thirst.

Create in us a community
who welcome weakness,
in covenant with Jesus.
You have given us to each other;
may we stay close enough to hear his heartbeat.

Jesus, we trust you,
gathered in your name;

you are here among us,
a stranger, Lord and friend.

Washing our feet,
you love us through to the end,
to transfigure your friends,
and embrace a covenant people.

O Spirit, we love you.
Renew our pilgrim hope.
And may we, though many,
become one,
deep in the heart of God.

Amen, shalom, amen.
From L'Arche Edinburgh

A pilgrim's prayer

Jesus,
Who was cradled in the arms of the Virgin Mary,
Enfold us in your life-giving love.

Jesus,
Who was embraced by the sinner and the slave,
Forgive us and set us free.

Jesus,
Who was handed over to be abused
And nailed to a cross,
Reach out your healing hands
And unite us in your peace.

Jesus,
Who has ascended to the Father's right hand,
Shower us with the Spirit's gifts,
So that our community
Will bear abundant fruit.
Amen.
From the Pilgrims Community

We care passionately about . . .

The Church

Small strength

Father,
make us worthy
to serve you.
Make us really lowly,
deeply humble
and full of love.

Make us small
so that no human name is honoured.
We want to honour Jesus alone.
Keep us in our small strength
so that the doors of heaven can open,
so that the power
of the blood of Christ,
the power of the forgiveness of sins,
can come to us.
Lead us all to be
a Church of small strength
so that the power of Jesus
can be victorious.
Amen.

From the Darvell Bruderhof

Covenanting together

Creating and redeeming God,
we give you thanks and praise for your covenant of grace
made for our salvation in Jesus Christ our Lord.
We come this day to covenant with you and with our fellow disciples
to watch over each other
and to walk together before you
in ways known and to be made known.

This day we give ourselves again to the Lord and to each other

to be bound together in fellowship,
for the sake of the mission and glory of God.
Celebrating our shared life,
we commit ourselves to belonging and working together
in our congregation, our local partnerships,
our Association, and our Union of churches.
We pledge all that we have
and all that we are
to fulfil God's purposes of love.
Amen.

From the Community of the Prince of Peace

A prayer for priests

Mary, beloved, make him all fire, filled with desire to warm the cold hearts of others.

Mary, beloved, give him the gift of tongues to speak of love that dies for love as if he were the lover.

Mary, beloved, pray to your Spouse, the Holy Spirit, that he will make him a mighty wind that lifts everyone to him who is, who was, and ever will be.

Mary, beloved, give him the gift of pain that sears and cleanses and makes whole again.

Mary, beloved, make him into another Christ, your Son.

From the Madonna House Community

The environment

The earth in mourning

Living Lord,
why do we turn from you to walk in selfish ways?
We have turned green fields into deserts;
we have felled rain forests and polluted rivers;
we have irradiated the air and fouled the seas;
we have called down judgement upon ourselves.

So we see devastation in our world:
hunger walks our streets and diseases inhabit our houses;
no one is immune; neither priests nor people,
neither employer nor employees,
neither seller nor buyer.
The earth is in mourning and the sound of merriment has gone.
Nor shall we sing again the song of celebration
until we turn to you, Lord God, and walk in your way.

From the Community for Reconciliation

The primal garden

Our Creator, Companion, Provider
who art in the Primal Garden,
we delight to offer love and honour to you,
the one who relates lovingly to us,
and who is described by glorious names.

May your garden come (and our vocation within it).

And may your permissions,
seen as freedoms offered within goodness,
be fulfilled
on earth as it was to have been in the First Garden.

Give us this day our regular provision, our holy sustenance,
the permissible bread-fruit;

And forgive us when we choose to follow our inner serpent-voice,
when we separate ourselves from you,
as we forgive those who have eaten the forbidden fruit,
who have harmed us and who have separated themselves from you.

Keep us from the delusion that there are no boundaries;
that we can be equal to you in knowledge, power and presence,
but save us from any trial that is beyond us.

Give us the strength to overcome
by knowing our vocations, our acceptable freedoms, our prohibitions.
May we recognise what is evil.

For yours is the Garden, the creative life-force, the grace and the glory.
Last time, this time, each time, times beyond time – thus we say forever!

Amen. Yes! Amen. Yes! AMEN!

From the Columbanus Community of Reconciliation

A prayer for planners

Lord God,
we have seen the blight
that can be caused in towns and cities by bad planning;
we recall the sufferings of generations in the slums;
we see how the same hardship is found in our own time.
May we be blessed with planners who have vision,
who plan villages, towns and cities
that encourage community care and mutual support.
May we learn the lessons of the past
as we plan for a future bright with promise
not for the chosen few but for all people.

From the Community for Reconciliation

Evangelisation

Why evangelise?

Jesus, why do I want to evangelise, to announce the Good News of the Kingdom? Why do I want to dedicate the whole of my life to spreading your Gospel to the ends of the earth? Why do I want to preach the Gospel of Jesus of Nazareth and consecrate myself to prayer and the ministry of the Word?

Because I want to bring good news to the afflicted, to soothe the broken-hearted, to proclaim liberty to captives, release to those in prison; so that the blind see again, and the lame walk, those suffering from virulent skin diseases are cleansed, the deaf hear, the dead are raised to life, and the Good News is proclaimed to the poor.

Because I long to change hate into love, sadness into joy, anguish and despair into optimism and hope, sickness and death into life and resurrection.

Because I am eager to see light dawn on gloomy faces, and shine into so many mournful hearts that lie in the shadow of death.

Because I want to give direction and meaning to so many paralysed lives, lives that are bored and lethargic, with doubts and suspicions, empty and broken by disabling complexes.

Because I see the urgent need for the Gospel to reach to the ends of the earth; to break the chains of those enslaved, crushed and oppressed by lack of culture and faith, even of food and shelter.

I want to inject with my own blood those who, in this delirium, renounce life and bury themselves alive. And shout to them all with the powerful voice of the Gospel:'Get up and live!'

I feel a passion to give the Gospel, alive and raw, to restless and rebellious young people who, dissatisfied and unconforming, protest against every-thing. I want to give them the sword of Truth as their defence. And to those of them who give up on life I want to shout with the powerful voice of the Gospel:'Young person, get up!'

A beautiful landscape is ready to be born: horizons radiant with light and hope, a new heaven and a new earth, when the Good News reaches these young people and informs their lives. I sincerely believe that seeing the fields ripen for the harvest is neither a fantasy nor a distant hope.

Why evangelise? Because I long for families to enjoy the warmth of a loving home, instead of the atmosphere almost of a cemetery, without even the embers of a fruitful and creative love, of intimacy, affection, care, spontaneity and joy.

I can't stop proclaiming the Good News of liberation, to save millions of children whose lives I see broken and disintegrated as soon as they open their eyes to the light or even in the very wombs of their mothers.

I am compelled to announce the Good News of the Kingdom of God, the Kingdom of peace and justice, the Kingdom of life and love, to stop the relentless war between nations and races, the painful conflicts between children and parents.

Then their children will be like new olive shoots around their table, and their hearts will overflow with more joy than over abundant corn and new wine.

I feel the need to give my life and pour out my blood for all people equally, regardless of sex, race and social condition.

Jesus, only your Gospel possesses the strength and power necessary to transform the misery that today corrupts these environments into the energy which generates abundant life. I know that with the Gospel the light of day will penetrate many homes which were in darkness.

That's why I can say, without any fear of being pretentious or of it being an abstract or unreasonable theory, that evangelising is for me a duty and a right, a joy and a complete and now irreversible dedication, as impossible for me to leave as it would be for me to renounce living, and renounce the fact that my brothers and sisters may have life and have it to the full.

Accompany me, Mary, with your most tender, motherly love, so that my consecration to the living Word of God and my preaching of it may be a continual propagation of God's life for all generations. Amen.

From the Verbum Dei Community

A prayer for the conversion of England

O Lord Jesus Christ,
High Priest and Victim,
You are the Lamb who was slain and has risen again.

By your most Precious Blood save your people
trapped in selfishness and sin.
To you who trampled death by your death we cry,
Jesus, convert England!

From the culture of death to your Gospel of life,
Jesus, convert England!

From the culture of fear and addiction
to the freedom of your children,
Jesus, convert England!

From the culture of disbelief, despair and greed
to the civilisation of faith, hope and love,
Jesus, convert England!

Uniting our prayers and our service with the offerings of the martyrs of this land, those who followed in your footsteps of self-sacrificing love without counting the cost, we pray that you would bring every heart to rejoice in you and in your gift of salvation, with the Holy Spirit, to the glory of God our Father. Amen.

From the Franciscan Friars of the Renewal

A mission prayer

Our Father in heaven,
We want to be like Jesus your Son
In all we think and say and do.
We want to put on the mind of Jesus,
Proclaim the Good News,
And serve those in greatest need.
May our faith in action be love,
And our love in action be service,
So that everyone we meet
Will see the beautiful things

Your Holy Spirit does through us
And will want to belong
To the wonderful world of your Kingdom.
Amen.

From the Pilgrims Community

Families and children

Mothers' prayers

The liturgy below may be used by small groups of mothers praying for their children. They may gather around a table on which is placed a candle, a Bible, and a cross with a small basket at its foot. Prayers may then be said …

… to invite the Holy Spirit.

Holy Spirit,
we welcome you here in our midst;
we thank you for your presence
and ask you to inspire us.

Please let this meeting be totally of the Lord.
Take away from us our thoughts
and replace them with your thoughts.

Give us the gift of praise,
to give glory, honour and worship to our God.

Give us the gift of intercession
so that we may bring our children before you,
seeking your will.

And give us the gift of heartfelt gratitude
for all the blessings you have bestowed upon them.
Amen.

… for protection.

Lord Jesus,
we ask you to bless, protect and cover each of us here
with your Precious Blood,
so that no evil will touch us or this house
as we humbly come before you
as concerned mothers to pray for our children.
Amen.

…for forgiveness.

Lord Jesus, we come before you, just as we are.
We are sorry for our sins. Please forgive us.
We give ourselves entirely to you, Lord Jesus.
We accept you as our Lord, God and Saviour.
Heal us, change us,
strengthen us in body, mind and spirit.
We love you, Lord Jesus.
We thank you, Lord Jesus.
We shall follow you every day of our lives.
Amen.

…for unity.

Lord, we repent of anything that
we may have against any one present here,
perhaps an unkind word or thought,
for no matter how small,
this may spoil the unity of our meeting.

We want to come to you, Lord,
in one heart and one mind.
So please unite us now, Lord Jesus,
with your love.
Thank you.
Amen.

A song of praise may be sung, followed by a prayer for unity with other groups of praying mothers:

Lord, we are serious in our requests.
We have wasted too much time worrying
and trying to put things right by ourselves
and even by doing nothing at all.

But now, Lord,
united with all our sisters in your family,
we praise and thank you
for the new hope you have given us,
as we bring our children to you.

A passage of Scripture may be read, followed by a prayer of thanksgiving for motherhood:

Thank you, dear Lord,
for the gift of motherhood.
This is such a blessed and dignified vocation.

Lord, we often forget
just how much you trust us
by giving one of your precious children
into our care.

Please help us always to appreciate
the importance of being a mother.

A final prayer may be said:

Lord Jesus, we come before you as mothers
wanting you to bless our children,
and all children throughout the world.

We thank you for our children –
they are a precious gift to us.
Help us, Lord, always to remember this,
especially when they are in difficulties.

Lord, they live in a troubled world,
a world that does not acknowledge you,
a world that may sometimes cause them to be laughed at
if they admit belief in you.
Help them to be strong, Lord.

Help us to know that you are always with us,
sharing in the joys and the sorrows,
joining us in the laughter,
and weeping with us in the pain.
Please give us all the graces we need
to fulfil your plans for our lives
and our duties in our families.

You are Almighty God.
You can change things.
So we turn to you in faith and love,
knowing that you will answer our prayers.
Lord, let us always remember

how much you love us and our children
and how you urge us to come to you with our problems.

The mothers may now, one by one, kneel or stand in front of the cross, and place the names of their children in the basket there. Other children, born or unborn, may be mentioned.

The meeting ends with a song of praise, a Glory Be, and the Lord's Prayer.

From the Solace Community

Fathers' prayer

Lord, we thank you for the gift of Fatherhood and ask forgiveness for our failure to carry out our responsibilities, our failure to love and our failure to protect our family.

We repent on behalf of all fathers and ask your help to turn away from the things that separate us from you.

We ask you, Lord, for the strength and guidance we need to fufil our role, to accept our proper place in society as fathers, following the example of Joseph, the husband of Mary.

We ask you, Father, for your protection of all women and children you have placed in our care and we ask you to guard them against all assaults of the enemy.

We ask this through you Son Jesus Christ our Lord.

Amen.

From the Solace Community

The mighty angels

Father, we ask you humbly
for the protection
of your good angels over all children,
over the newborn,
over all the children
who are here in this room,
or wherever they are.

We ask you for your care
and protection
of the sick ones.

Father, we thank you for your help
through the mighty angels
who do your will.
Amen.
From the Darvell Bruderhof

The miserable child

how then to approach the miserable child
      not haughtily
           but humbly
      not judging but loving
           determined not to dominate
           not even to give things
           rather to give myself
                my time
                        energy
                and heart

and to listen
      believing that he is important
           a child of God
                in whom Jesus lives

approach with tenderness
      gently

gently giving one's friendship
      delicate soothing hands
           bearing the oil of mercy
                anointing deep wounds.
From L'Arche Lambeth

The children

The cry
of my little ones
pierces the air.
The shriek
of the innocents
is now heard

from afar.
Their call
for our help
has gone unheeded
for long
we have heard
but not listened to
their plaintive requests,
and our deafening
silence
can no longer
remain
as God shatters
our apathy
and coldness
of heart
and demands
that we speak
for the children
who are weak
and lost
and bruised
and lonely,
for they
are his
and beyond
all price.

From the Maranatha Community

One family

Dear Lord,
with Mary and Joseph,
you have lived within a family.
Teach me always to appreciate
the precious gift of being part of a family.

Show me ever new ways to protect
and comfort those closest to me,
and let me each day do something that will say
'I love you' without speaking the words.
But remind me frequently to say those words.

Let me never part from any member of my family in anger.
Prompt me always to turn back without delay
to forgive and be forgiven.

Let me see your image within each person,
in my own family and in my greater family,
knowing that in your kingdom
we will truly be one family,
united by your sacrifice on the Cross.

From the Solace Community

A cup of rice

It is easier to give a cup of rice to relieve hunger
than to relieve the loneliness and pain
of someone unloved in our own home.

From the Missionaries of Charity

Wind the thread

Wind the thread of hope, Lord, and bind the thread of joy.
Wind the thread of kindness, Lord, and bind the thread of love.
Wind the thread of patience, Lord, and bind the thread of peace.
When we are bound to you, Lord, we find the thread of life.

From the Community for Reconciliation

Thank you for our day

*This is a family's prayer at night with children. Pause after each line to draw a
deep breath and to breathe out, remembering the events of the day together.*

Thank you for our day,
And sorry for times that were hard.
Please help us all to live in peace and love.

From L'Arche Edinburgh

Healing

A door of hope

The Vale of Achor is the valley of misfortune
a dangerous valley close to Jericho
an accursed place
swarming with insects and poisonous creatures
a place to flee
a place of pain
a place of your pain
a place to avoid
to dread
to keep out of
to try to forget
a place of the poor, suffering, desperate and disinherited
those you avoid
reject, hide
try to forget about
And yet God says:
'I will make the Vale of Achor
a door of hope' (Hosea 2:15)
That is the mystery: God says
if you do not run away
if you dare to enter the place of pain
within your own heart
if you welcome
those you fear
those you reject
those who threaten you
because they are poor and weak and wounded
among them the wounded child within you:
the child who you shut away
behind a high wall
long ago:
if you welcome that child
and welcome yourself
you will be on the road to healing

and the Vale of Achor
will become a door of hope.

From L'Arche Lambeth

A liturgy for healing the land

*Healing the land brings the Church's healing ministry to bear on the
environment and on communal memory.*

Meditation:

Jesus' resurrection was physical as well as spiritual. It involved a healing pattern that affected matter, including bones. God wants to treat life as an organic whole. Through his resurrection, Jesus was made Lord over all creation, and all enemies are now under his feet. This includes the enemy of the original curse upon the land resulting from Adam's sin. The resurrection touches all times, places and elements. Christians are to share Jesus' rule, which extends not only to believers, but to the whole universe. We share this rule with the one whom 'the winds and the waves obey' not by our own power but as channels of the Spirit. Thus the gifts which were meant for humans from the beginning of creation, but were lost, such as the power to bless, were restored through the resurrection of Jesus. Healing is not only repairing; it is a new creation.

*People are asked beforehand to bring quite a large stone from the locality. Each
now holds their stone, which represents some sin from the communal memory.*
  There may be singing.

Leader   We name the dark practices, the selfish deeds, the shame or
            neglect which we believe this place has imbibed …

*Each person names the sin which their stone represents, and places it in a heap
in the midst of the gathering.*

Leader   In sorrow we bring these to you.
            We acknowledge the wrong, and we ask you to forgive.

*The leader brings water from a baptistry, font, well or tap, blesses it, and pours it
over the stones with words such as these:*

            In the name of the holy and almighty God,
            May the cleansing power of the Creator,

The cleansing blood of the Saviour,
And the cleansing water of the Spirit
Wash over the sins of time,
The deeds of shame, the thoughts that destroy.

Now a cross is placed in the ground amid the stones.

Leader   We plant the Cross of Christ in the soil of our shame. May Christ
set this land free from the power of the past to control the
present, from the bitterness of memories.

All   **May healing take place.**
May wholeness be restored.
May this be heavenly ground.

From the Community of Aidan and Hilda

Unlock our hearts

May oppressed people, and those who oppress them, free each other.
May those who are handicapped, and those who think they are not, help each
other.
May those who need someone to listen touch the hearts of those who are
too busy.
May the homeless bring joy to those who open their doors reluctantly.
May the lonely heal those who think they are self-sufficient.
May the poor melt the hearts of the rich.
May seekers for truth give life to those who are satisfied that they have found
it.
May the dying who do not wish to die be comforted by those who find it hard
to live.
May the unloved be allowed to unlock the hearts of those who cannot
love.
May prisoners find true freedom and liberate others from fear.
May those who sleep on the streets share their gentleness with those who
cannot understand them.
May the hungry tear the veil from the eyes of those who do not hunger after
justice.
May those who live without hope cleanse the hearts of their brothers and
sisters who are afraid to live.
May the weak confound the strong and save them.
May violence be overcome by compassion.
May violence be absorbed my men and women of peace.

May violence succumb to those who are totally vulnerable.

That we might be healed.

From L'Arche Lambeth

Bring together

Bring together and mend,
mend and forever preserve
what here lies broken.

From the Hengrave Community

Healing   153

Peace

A prayer for Hiroshima Day

An atomic bomb was dropped on Hiroshima on 6 August 1945.

The words in bold may be said all together.

God, today in sorrow we remember and we share our grief.

The few seconds of annihilating time
at Hiroshima and Nagasaki that seared itself forever
into the depth of our present existence.
Those who died, those who wish they had died
and those who live never to forget:
> **we remember**

The many thousands all over the world
who sighed with relief at the ending
of six long years of war.
Those who died,
those whose sufferings made them long for death,
those whose experiences seared their lives
and hopes forever,
those who waited, mourned,
and lived lives of regret at home:
> **we remember**

The scientists, politicians, engineers, technicians
and members of the armed forces
who came to realise the awesome power and
responsibility of new technology,
and who live with the results of that knowledge;
> **we remember**

The present generation,
growing up in a changed world
overshadowed by the threat of extinction,
feeling helpless in the web of events:
> **we remember**

We acknowledge our share of the pain and the responsibility.
God, in Christ you showed us
that you are not removed from us
but share in our agony and suffering.
You are the mother holding her child from the blast,
you are the tortured prisoner longing for release,
you are the war-weary soldier,
you are the scientist pacing the midnight hour,
you are the child with nuclear nightmares,
you know and suffer our human condition.

We know that nothing can separate us from your love.
We pray for your love to enfold us in comfort
your love to share our agony
your love to inspire us to love one another
your love to live in hope.

From the Iona Community

True safety

Holy Lord,
what shall we do when all around us
people enter into a covenant with death,
making missiles of destruction, building underground shelters
inventing their theology of escape
and claiming a place of safety for the day of annihilation?

But you, Lord, have given us our only true safety;
you have given us a Saviour who stands for justice,
who seeks to establish the right.
In the structure of the world, he is the precious cornerstone;
in him we trust, and our trust will not be in vain.

From the Community for Reconciliation

Your peace

God of harmony,
when the nations seek peace
they make their treaties and alliances.
There is peace of a kind
but it is subject to betrayals and denials;

there is still a lack of brotherhood and love.
But your peace goes deeper.
Your peace draws together people with their neighbours.
Your peace makes us one with you.
Your peace is sacrificial love
   which recognises the good in all people,
   stands out against injustice and oppression
   and frees people to realise their full potential.
Your peace is health and holiness,
   it is wholeness and salvation.
May we find our peace through Jesus Christ our Lord.

From the Community for Reconciliation

The beginning

Peace begins with a smile.

From the Missionaries of Charity

The poor

Two prisons

the miserable man
i treat you as a stranger ...
you were born and reared in squalor
you are walled in,
for you have no life
in front of you ... no joys to look
forward to ... no loving children ...
no esteem

t w o   p r i s o n s   d i v i d e d   b y   a   g u l f

i, with my clean clothes, my
sensitive nose (i hate bad smells)
my politeness ... a warm house
a world of security ... the light
of reality does not penetrate my
cell, the reality of human misery
so widespread, so deep ...

two prisons divided by a gulf: the miserable man ...
and, imprisoned in the cell next door, the man of means
comfortably installed ... and so the world goes on,
and the gulf gets wider

who will be the bridge

From L'Arche Lambeth

For the hungry

The words in bold may be said all together.

Let us pray for those who hunger in this land:
whose only kitchen is a soup kitchen,
whose only food is what others don't want,
whose diet depends on luck, not on planning.

Pause.

Lord, feed your people
using our skills and conscience,
and eradicate from our policies and private lives
the apathy to hunger which comes from over-eating.

Let us pray for the hungry and the fed.
> **Lord, have mercy.**

Let us pray for the hungry in other lands,
where economies, burdened by debt,
cannot respond to human need;
or where fields are farmed for our benefit
by low-waged workers courted by starvation.

Pause.

Lord, feed our people,
even if rulers must cancel debt,
and shareholders lose profit,
or diners restrict their choice
in order that all may be nourished.

Let us pray for the hungry and the fed.
> **Lord, have mercy.**

Let us pray for the hungry for justice,
who document inequalities,
demonstrate against tyranny,
distinguish between need and greed,
and are sometimes misrepresented or persecuted in the process.

Pause.

May their labour not be in vain
and may we be counted in their number.

Let us pray for the hungry and the fed.
> **Lord, have mercy.**

So, in the presence of the Bread of Life,
who refused food for himself

in order to nourish others,
we deepen our devotion by praying his words:

Our Father ...

From the Iona Community

If we pray

If we pray
   we will believe.
If we believe
   we will love.
If we love
   we will serve.
Only then can we put
   our love for God
   into living action
through service of Christ
   in the distressing
   disguise of the poor.

From the Missionaries of Charity

The question of property

Father,
Let us carry the hungry of the world
On our hearts, so that our
Financial resources are used
Only for the building up of a
Brotherly life and for
The need of the hungry.

Lead us rightly in the question of
Property so that we not only have no
Private property, but also that the
Communal property is not collected
In a wrong way.
Amen.

From the Darvell Bruderhof

The exiles in our midst

God beyond borders
we bless you for strange places and different dreams
for the demands and diversity of a wider world
for the distance that lets us look back and re-evaluate
for new ground where broken stems can take root, grow and blossom.
We bless you for the friendship of strangers
the richness of other cultures
and the painful gift of freedom.
Blessed are you, God beyond borders.
But if we have overlooked the exiles in our midst
heightened their exclusion by our indifference
given our permission for a climate of fear
and tolerated a culture of violence,
have mercy on us.
God who takes side with justice
confront our prejudice
stretch our narrowness
sift out our laws and our lives
with the penetrating insight
of your Spirit
until generosity is our only measure.
Amen.
       From the Iona Community

Poverty

Make me poor, Lord.
Help me discard
all pretensions,
the lies
of self-sufficiency
and sweet success,
to set aside
the restless seeking
for self-fulfilment,
to abandon
each desire
to possess
to gain

to hold.
Give me now
the gift of poverty
of mind and spirit
that my sole hunger
may be for
your truth
and goodness
and beauty
and love,
and then
in my
unencumbered lowliness
I will be rich.

From the Maranatha Community

Furs and fast cars

Mother of all creation,
help us to see how we have betrayed you;
when for vanity we wear rich jewels whilst children starve;
when for pride we drive fast cars whilst refugees lack a home;
when for fashion we buy furs and whole species are endangered;
when we drink wine and bottled minerals whilst many lack pure water.

Mother of all creation, pour out your Spirit upon us
that the desert may be irrigated and become a place of lush vegetation,
that there may be justice and righteousness in the wilderness
and, springing from them, trust and peace in the fruitful field.

So may your people come to the place of reconciliation
and all live secure together, the animals, the people,
in a place of pure streams and quiet fields of peace.

From the Community for Reconciliation

So much more

Let us not be satisfied
    with just giving money.
Money is not enough.

From the Missionaries of Charity

Our most precious jewel

Our beloved Father in heaven,
grant that we experience and feel
in our hearts,
in absolute genuineness,
a longing for you.

Our longing is to be poor
and to thirst for you.

Grant that we do not gather material
things on earth, but that our goal,
our most precious jewel,
is in heaven.

Let us fight for you.
We know that each repentance is a
victory for your kingdom.
We ask you, make us lowly and
real children and fighters for you.
Amen.

From the Darvell Bruderhof

Sanctity of life

The Gospel of life

O Mary, bright dawn of the new world, Mother of the living, to you do we entrust the cause of life: look down, O Mother, upon the vast number of babies not allowed to be born, of the poor whose lives are made difficult, of men and women who are victims of brutal violence, of the elderly and the sick killed by indifference or out of misguided mercy.

Grant that all who believe in your Son may proclaim the Gospel of life with honesty and love to the people of our time. Obtain for them the grace to accept that Gospel as a gift ever new, the joy of celebrating it with gratitude throughout their lives and the courage to bear witness to it resolutely, in order to build, together with all people of good will, the civilisation of truth and love, to the praise and glory of God, the Creator and lover of life.

From the Sisters of the Gospel of Life

Truth

We are called

We are called
to deny the lie
that there can be
a Kingdom without a King
that there can be
peace without the Prince of Peace
that there can be wisdom
without the Spirit who is truth
that there can be love
without the King of Love
that there can be a flock
without the Shepherd
that there can be a family
without a Father
that there can be forgiveness
without a Cross
that there can be justice
without the Eternal Judge.
We are called to deny
that truth and falsehood
can together reign,
that humankind
is the master of its fate.
We are called to warn
that there is a price to be paid
for believing
or even half-believing
the cunning wily lies
of the one who is
the father of lies.
We are called to proclaim
the victory of Christ
over all deception
over all that is not true
over all the powers of

darkness
– here and now
and with no more delay.

From the Maranatha Commmunity

The brightness of truth

Almighty God,
in whose prophets through the ages
we have seen the brightness of your truth,
we pray for people of vision in our day,
those who carry undimmed
the light of the longing for justice,
those who speak in the councils of nations
to persuade and convince,
those who give leadership and support to action groups,
networks and political parties,
those who resist blind power and risk persecution
to show a new way.

We pray for people in the front line of change,
all who are called to explore our common future,
editors, politicians, poets and pundits,
prophets of speech and pen, canvas and lens,
artists who are not afraid to look
and tell what they see,
who name what is deadly
and call us to new birth,
who trust their imagination
so that we may live life to the full.

From the Iona Community

The living word

Our Father in heaven,
we ask you, touch our hearts
with the finger of your Holy Spirit,
and write
the living word
out of your mouth
into our hearts.

Grant that we understand
the living and complete Gospel,
that we change nothing,
bend nothing,
decorate nothing,
but proclaim it as if Christ's heart
burns in our hearts.
Amen.

> *From the Darvell Bruderhof*

Come the day

In the following prayer, two groups can alternate on each line.

Come the day
        and I will send upon the land
Not a hunger for bread
        or a thirst for water,
But a yearning to hear
        the word of God,
A famine that I have planned:
        Come the day!

> *From L'Arche Edinburgh*

God's thunder

There is a time
for silence, Lord,
but not
when deeds are done
which shame
extremest hell.
There is a time
for withholding
my words, Lord,
but not
when the lie
goes unchallenged
and foulest acts accepted.
There is a time
for my lips

to remain
tightly sealed,
but not
when the devil
lets loose his powers
to degrade and destroy
to twist and pervert
the young, the lonely
the poor, the vulnerable.
There is a time
when my voice
must be raised
to speak out
with your words
upon my lips.
For you, O Lord
are not a God
of perpetual silence.
You roar
against the tyrant.
You thunder
against iniquity
and at the sound
of your voice
the nations tremble.

From the Maranatha Community

Unity

A prayer for unity in Christ

Lord Jesus,
who on the eve of your death
prayed that all your disciples might be one,
as you in the Father and the Father in you,
make us feel intense sorrow
over the infidelity of our disunity.

Give us the honesty to recognise,
and the courage to reject,
whatever indifference towards one another,
or mutual distrust, or even enmity,
lie hidden within us.

Enable us to meet one another in you.
And let your prayer for the unity of Christians
be ever in our hearts and on our lips,
unity such as you desire
and by the means that you will.

Make us find the way
that leads to unity in you,
who are perfect charity,
through being obedient
to the Spirit of love and truth.
Amen.
> *From the Cornerstone Community*

More than any other treasure

If we are united, Jesus is among us. And this has value. It is worth more than any other treasure that our heart possesses; more than mother, father, brothers, sisters, children. It is worth more than our house, our work, or our property; more than the works of art in a great city like Rome; more than our business deals; more than nature which surrounds us with flowers and fields, the sea and the stars; more than our soul.

From the Focolare Movement

The instinct of the Holy Spirit

Our Father in heaven,
we thank you for your goodness,
for how you are leading us together.

We ask you
that we may live in the will of God
in all things and that
you may give us
the instinct of the Holy Spirit
so that when we depart
from your will and your atmosphere
and your Spirit
we feel it.

Grant this also
in the area of sports and games
so that
joyful, harmonious playing
can be given
without worldly competition
and sinfulness.
Amen.

From the Darvell Bruderhof

The diamond

Father, make the unity we pray for a reality by banishing from our minds the attitudes of division; from our hearts the causes of discord; and from our actions the display of selfishness.

May the Body of Christ become like a diamond that shimmers his love-light to all from its many facets, and not remain a mirror, broken and plundered, shattered, which can only scatter your light.

May your Spirit, holy and joyful, set us all to the task of oneness that cannot be accomplished without you. Through Christ the living Lord. Amen.

From the Hengrave Community

Make us all one

Jesus,
come close, very close to us,
and unite us
as it is and always was your will.
Make us all one
because the hand of your Spirit
goes deep, deep into all hearts.
When we are all one,
your will can happen.

From the Darvell Bruderhof

To experience the suffering

Lord Jesus,
who prayed that we might all be one,
we pray to you for the unity of Christians,
according to your will,
according to your means.
May your Spirit enable us
to experience the suffering caused by division,
to see our sin,
and to hope beyond all hope.

From the Chemin Neuf Community

Together

Coals on a fire,
Flowers in a garden,
Birds in formation,
Stars in the sky,
Pebbles on the seashore,
Sounds from an orchestra.
Lord, you want us each
To be what we were made for,
But you love it
When we 'be' it
Together!

From the House of the Open Door

Especially for young people

Jericho

I walk the walls of Jericho from morn to night.
Not a word escapes my lips in the falling of the light.

When will the Ram's horn blow?
When will the first stone roll?
When will the soldiers shout,
and in the thunder of the falling stones
let this captive out?

I walk the walls of Jericho from day to day:
walls so high they're out of sight,
but there has to be a way.

I've been a captive oh so long in these walls of grey;
the stones of fear and isolation keep my loved ones away.

Not a soul comes out of there and not a soul comes in.
These are the walls of my poor heart that are built by my sin.

My Joshua, my Jesus, won't you rescue me?
There's so much treasure deep inside me only you can see.

I'd give it all to you,
feed your lambs and feed your sheep.
All the gold and silver in my city walls
I would give to you to keep.

And when the walls are broken
I will call you inside,
give you all the love that I have
always tried to hide.
            From the Pilgrims Community

Do I dare?

listening
l i s t e n i n g
l i s t e n i n g

         whispering
         silent
         a listening that comforts
             and calls forth

DO I DARE
do i dare
    believe
        your silent call
        your tears of silence

but there is a world of efficiency
        techniques
        diplomas
        business (and business is business!)

and then there are my friends
    who think i'm crazy … are they friends?
        am i crazy?
… DOUBTS …

conflicting forces
    fatigue
    fears

and yet life calls forth
    compassion in my entrails

this strange and silent war
    do i dare
    do i dare
        believe
    do i dare
    do i dare

    surrender myself to your call

From L'Arche Lambeth

Heart speaks to heart

This prayer should be said very slowly. It aims to take you and Jesus to your quiet place, where you can talk, or just sit and be.

Jesus, come into my heart now.
I give you permission to enter my life and my soul.
Come, Lord Jesus, come.

Pause.

Take from me, Lord, any distracting thoughts or anxieties.
Take my worries about …

(Here you can place your present concerns, or what is most on your mind.)

I leave them at the foot of your cross.

Pause, and imagine leaving this thing or person at the foot of the cross.

Jesus, I desire you in this present moment.
Come, Lord, with your light and love.
Come deeply into my soul.
Come into the place where no one else can go.
Come into that hidden place where only you and I are at home.

Come, Lord Jesus, come. *Pause.*
Come, Lord Jesus, come. *Pause.*
Come, Lord Jesus, come. *Pause.*

And now we are alone.
All is quiet and still, and I am with the one whom I love.
Jesus, to look and be with you is enough.
Let me look at you for a moment.

In your heart, gaze on the loving face of Jesus; look into his eyes and receive his love.

Thank you, Jesus, for being here now.

Now speak to Jesus, praying in your own words. Say what is on your mind. Ask

for his help. Or perhaps you will simply want to be with Jesus, drawing strength
from his presence in your soul.

Thank you, Jesus, for this time with you. It is time for me to go.
I know you will be with me as I leave now.
You have made me a tabernacle of your light.
Help me, Lord, to reflect your presence to all those I meet today,
that I may be a living temple of love.
Be with me, Lord.
I praise you, Lord, and thank you for your love.
Praise you, Jesus; I love you, Jesus.

Glory be to the Father, Son and Holy Spirit.
As it was in the beginning, is now and ever shall be, world without end.
Amen.
    From Youth 2000

Is there anything I can do?

*This piece is dedicated to the street children of Guatemala who have suffered so
much, and also to those brave enough to help them. The indented verses could
be spoken by a second reader, or by everyone together.*

I heard they kill the children on the streets now,
Just because they didn't like them there.
I heard they left them dying in the sunlight,
Cos society doesn't care.

    Is there anything you can do to help them?
    Is there anything you can say?
    Is there anything you can do to take them
    safely out of there?

In the West we don't kill them quickly;
we kill their souls instead.
All they want is some love and affection.
We'd give them anything instead.

    Is there anything you can do to heal them?
    Is there anything you can say?
    Is there anything you can do to show them
    how to live your way?

I heard the news and I read the paper.
They left me cold inside.
All around me I saw hate and confusion,
Till a voice inside me cried:

> Why don't you come and stop the bleeding?
> Why don't you set us free?
> Why don't you come and heal the heartache?
> Why don't you answer me?

Once again I saw the children dying.
I saw the blood run red.
Once again I heard the people crying,
But with your voice instead,
you said:

> 'My blood is the blood of all the wounded.
> My tears flow with those who weep.
> My soul is in pain with all the dying,
> and I give you a harvest to reap.'

I looked and found my hands were hands of kindness.
My words were made to heal.
I looked to find my heart overflowing
to see your truth revealed.
I cried:

> Is there anything I can do to save them?
> Is there anything I can say?
> Is there anything I can do to show them
> how to live your way?

I'll show them how to live your way.
From the Pilgrims Community

Seasons of love

Spring
> Sometimes
> You beckon me,
> Your love interrupts,
> Disturbs, excites me.

I'll climb mountains,
Cross seas,
Run no matter where
To be with you.

Summer
Sometimes,
There are no words
But just a meeting.
As the sun soaks,
I'm love-bathed.
The running stops,
And I am here
Resting in you.

Autumn
Sometimes,
Like a bride leans,
I need to confide,
To consult, to hear you.
Your arm supports me,
Your words are intimate,
Your faithfulness
Holds me tenderly.

Winter
Sometimes,
I am without,
And all I know
Is unbearable
Absence,
Showing me how huge
Is the space
You fill
In me.
From the House of the Open Door

Come

He says
Come
to me.

Come
with your heavy load.
Come
with your tiredness.
Come
with all your guilt.
Come
with your regrets.
Come
with your hurts,
your bruises
and your pain.
Come
close to me.
Feel
my embrace,
my breath
upon your life.
Come
as you are,
now.
Allow my heart
to beat
within you.
Come, see
my outstretched arms.
Come
end my waiting.
Come home
to me.

From the Maranatha Community

Been with Jesus

'I've been with Jesus,'
   My old friend would say,
And you know, Lord, your fragrance
   Hung around her,

As it clings to others
   Who give you time each day,

Their love for you
   Growing stronger.

To be with Jesus
   Is to really live.
His presence transforms
   Our day.

It's a secret that's held
   Inside ourselves,
But his scent gives it
   Away!

From the House of the Open Door

Prayer before the Blessed Sacrament

Jesus, I believe that you are truly present here now,
but my heart is full of doubts and uncertainties.
Jesus, I know that you loved me into being so that I could know you.
Take me into the depths of your heart so that I may experience your love for me.
Draw me deeper into the mystery of your presence here.

In your presence, Lord, I become aware of my inadequacies.
Your radiant light, which penetrates the depths of my being,
shows up the darkness of my sin.
Cleanse me, Jesus, with your purifying fire.
Wash me clean, that I may stand before you without shame.

Jesus, your grace flows out to me in abundance.
Allow me to receive all that you have prepared for me,
so that I may become the person that you created me to be.
Help me, Jesus, to be a radiant witness to your love,
to work unceasingly to bring your message of love to all I meet.

From Youth 2000

Epilogue:
Come, Lord Jesus

Maranatha – Come, Lord Jesus

You are the God
who comes.
You do not
stay away.
You are not
afar off.
You come to me
often unawares,
gently entering
my life
to share
my joys, my pains.
You come
as an unseen guest
at every meal.
You come,
my companion
on every journey.
You come,
watching over me
in sleep at night.
You come
to share my life,
not to intrude,
nor to impose your will.
You come
with tenderness
and love
to share
and care
and listen,
to assure me
that I am not
alone,
living my life

in isolation.
You come,
the mighty one,
and knock
on the poor door
of my heart
persistently,
patiently,
lovingly.
You will not force
your entrance
or batter down
the door of
my stubborn resistance.
You stand,
you wait
at the door
you have chosen.
You have come
that I might have
life
in all its
abundance.
You have taken
the initiative.
You have drawn
close.
You come,
calling my name,
seeking
to touch me,
seeking
to breathe on me,
seeking
to give me
your Spirit
that I might be
healed.
You come
to share
my life
and being.
You come

in silence,
yearning
for my response,
waiting
for my 'Yes'.
Almighty God,
beyond my grasp,
towering high
in all infinity,
you do not always come
in grandeur,
pomp and
glorious splendour.
You come
as a little child,
helpless,
poor
and weak,
sharing my
humanity
in Jesus.
You come
speaking
my language.
You come
sharing
my pain.
You come
with arms
stretched out
to heal
and save,
with arms
stretched out
upon a cross,
and in the
darkest hour
you come
to bear
my burdens
and
the heavy load
of an agonising

world
crushed
with anguish,
guilt and grief.
Thank you
for coming, Lord,
and in your mercy
keep coming, Lord.
Come and
tread the streets
of cruel cities.
Come and
share the pain
of bloody
battlefields.
Come and
cry out for food
with those who
starve.
Come and
weep with all the
little ones,
abused, rejected
and alone.
Come, our Lord,
and lead us
out of darkness
into light.
Come, my Lord
and walk
with me
and reign
in me
and over all
the earth.
Come, Lord Jesus.
Come.
Amen.

From the Maranatha Community

Who we are

The communities are arranged below in alphabetical order, using key words. For example, the Community of St Fursey may be found under the letter 'f'.

The Community of Aidan and Hilda

The community is a body of Christians who seek to heal the land and cradle a spirituality for today. It welcomes people from all Churches and countries who wish to be wholly available to the holy Trinity, and to the way of Jesus as revealed to us in the Bible.

In the earthing of that commitment, members draw inspiration from the Celtic saints such as Aidan and Hilda: Aidan, the people's saint who brought Christianity to English-speakers through love, not fear; Hilda, pioneer of women's ministry, trainer of evangelists, encourager of overlooked folk, mother of the Church. Together these two are a sign of soul friends of different race and gender working together for the common good.

Members follow a Way of Life, with a soul friend, based on prayer, study, simplicity, care for creation and mission. They seek to renew the Church by weaving together the separated Catholic, Reformed, Orthodox and Pentecostal strands, and by fostering a new kind of monasticism.

The community began in 1994 and has members on four continents, including a USA order. It is served by a Caim ('encircling') Council and by its guardian, the Revd. Ray Simpson. It has advisors from different church streams, and the community soul friend is Bishop Ian Harland. It has a quarterly magazine, produces resources for individuals and churches, and has a house of prayer at Leek in Staffordshire.

Contact address and retreat house: The Open Gate, Holy Island, Berwick-upon-Tweed TD15 2SD. Tel. 01289 389222; Fax. 01289 389378.
e-mail: community@theopengate.ndo.co.uk
website: www.aidan. org.uk

The Bowthorpe Ecumenical Community

In 1974 the new development of Bowthorpe began to arise on the outskirts of Norwich. It consists of three urban villages, which meet at the shopping and social centre. Six Churches (the Quaker, Methodist, Anglican, Catholic, United Reformed and Baptist Churches) formed a Local Ecumenical Partnership, and agreed that they should establish one family of Christians for one neighbourhood. It would be called 'The Christian Church in Bowthorpe'.

Church members have developed a Work and Worship Area with the logo 'A heart for the community'. In the worship centre, united worship on Sunday combines the four essentials found in the early Church's worship: praise, prayer, the Word of God and the breaking of bread. A Catholic mass is celebrated on Saturday night. Ecumenical, meditative Morning Praise and Evening Prayer take place every weekday, punctuated on two evenings by an informal prayer meeting (Wednesday) and Taizé prayer around the cross (Friday).

Bowthorpe's vision is 'The Community for Christ', both in the sense of making Christ known, and in creating a neighbourhood where all that goes on can be offered to him. Near the worship centre are wood-workshops for the disadvantaged, a drop-in craft shop and a retreat cottage, all sponsored by Bowthorpe Community Trust, which is linked to the church. A cell for private prayer, dedicated to St Walstan, stands close by, accessible to all who go past, including children. It plays a part in turning the unconscious life of the neighbourhood Godwards.

Contact address: 2a St Michael's Cottages, Bowthope, Norwich NR5 9AA. Tel. 01603 745698.

The Chemin Neuf Community

The community was founded in France in 1973 and was shaped by the Charismatic Renewal and Ignatian sprituality. It now has houses in 19 countries and is present in another 20 countries.

It is a Catholic community with an ecumenical vocation, one in which members of different Christian denominations commit their lives. It is made up of men and women (single, celibate or married) united by their faith in Jesus Christ and a common desire to serve the Church, the Gospel and the world.

Around 600 members live in household fraternities or neighbourhood fraternities. They make a commitment to share their lives, to support various missions, to live in submission to each other, and to rely on the grace of the Holy Spirit and the providence of God.

Missions include work with couples (CANA), teenagers and youth, welcome ministries and the animation of parishes. These missions use formation programmes based on Ignatian spirituality whose main elements are the Spiritual Exercises, catechetical and biblical training, and reflection on important questions concerning the Church and contemporary issues.

Actively supporting this work is the Chemin Neuf Communion, comprising about 6,000 members worldwide.

The house in England is owned by the Sisters of Christian Instruction and was entrusted to the community in September 1999. The community here has seven English members, all Anglican. Members from other countries help to run the house, which has a ministry of welcome and openness to parishes, as well as organising language courses for people who want to learn English.

Contact address: St Gildas Christian Centre, The Hill, Langport, Somerset TA10 9QF. Tel. 01458 250496.

The Clare Priory Community

Clare Priory dates back to 1248, when it became the first foundation of the Augustinian (Austin) Friars in England. The friars subsequently spread throughout England and Ireland. After the Reformation, they became extinct in England but survived in Ireland, returning to London in the middle of the nineteenth century, and eventually to Clare Priory in 1953.

After some years as a house of training for aspirants, the Priory began to take on a new role in the 1980s as a retreat house and community of welcome. This developed into a mixed community of friars and laity living according to the Rule of St Augustine of Hippo, while engaged in retreat work and running the local Catholic parish. Lay members can be of either sex, and for a time included a married couple. Also belonging to the community are those who are closely associated with the Priory but are not residents.

The Rule of St Augustine emphasises the search for God in common, which is the primary inspiration of the community. Retreat guests are invited to participate in the life of the house by joining in its common prayer and eating at the same table as the community. Members are also available to guests who may wish spiritual direction or just a listening ear.

As well as the Rule, a source of inspiration is devotion to Mary, Mother of Good Counsel, to whom the Priiory is dedicated. This Marian devotion is common in many Augustinian churches, originating in the shrine of the same name at Genazzano, near Rome. There is a small shrine in a fifteenth-century, half-timbered part of the Priory, where people come and pray for guidance, advice and good counsel. Christians of all denominations visit the Priory, where much informal ecumenical dialogue takes place.

Contact address: Clare Priory, Clare, Sudbury, Suffolk CO10 8NX. Tel. 01787 277326.

Coleg Trefeca

Coleg Trefeca is the former home of Howell Harris, a prominent leader of the Methodist revival movement in Wales in the eighteenth century. The main building was erected, at Harris' direction, to house a remarkable Christian community, known as Teulu Trefeca, which means 'Trefeca family'. At its height, more than one hundred lay men, women and children lived at Trefeca. On joining, new members were required to sell all their possessions and contribute their worth to the common purse. The community followed a strict discipline of work and worship, rising at 4.00 a.m. to begin the day with prayer. More than 70 different trades were practised, including farming, clock– and furniture-making, and the printing of books. Teulu Trefeca was therefore virtually self-sufficient.

Today, Coleg Trefeca is a centre for training, conferences and retreats, owned by the Presbyterian Church of Wales but used widely ecumenically. A resident community comprises the joint wardens and their young children, and the assistant warden.

A wider, dispersed community, 'Teulu Trefeca' (named after the original Trefeca community), unites in prayer using the daily Teulu Devotions, meets at regular Teulu events and keeps in touch via a newsletter. Teulu Trefeca exists both to support the work of Coleg Trefeca in practical ways and to inspire and encourage its members on their own Christian journey of discipleship in the place where they live.

Contact address: Coleg Trefeca, Trefeca, Brecon, Powys LD3 0PP.
Tel. 01874 711423
e-mail: trefeca@surfaid.org
Coleg Trefeca, Trefeca, Aberhonddu, Powys LD3 0PP. Ffôn. 01874 711423.
ebost: trefeca@surfaid.org

The Columbanus Community of Reconciliation

The community comprises men and women from different Christian Churches, married and single, lay and ordained. We are committed in all aspects of our life to reconciliation in and through Christ, according to Jesus' prayer 'that they may be one as we are one … so that the world may believe'.

The residential community is at the heart of the Columbanus Family of Reconciliation, a growing circle of Christians from a variety of traditions who seek both to reconcile and to celebrate the diversity they represent, and to challenge the divisions within and between the Churches. The Columbanus Family takes its inspiration from the community, which in turn draws on the spiritual and practical resources available in the wider family.

Inspired by Michael Hurley SJ, founder of the Irish School of Ecumenics, the community was established in Belfast in November 1983, with the endorsement and active involvement of Anglican, Catholic, Methodist and Presbyterian church leaders.

It affords a setting in which Catholics, Anglicans and Protestants can share lives of prayer and service, witnessing to their desire for the uniting of all Christian Churches as the one Body of Christ. Members are committed to educating themselves and others on the issues that unite and divide the Churches. In our role as reconcilers, we offer hospitality to any who come to the door. We also conduct or host programmes to enhance mutual understanding and spiritual growth. By its presence and participation, the community also supports inter-church and cross-community work for unity, justice and peace throughout Northern Ireland.

Contact address: 683 Antrim Road, Belfast, Northern Ireland, BT15 4EG. Tel. 028 90 778009.

The Cornerstone Community

In the late 1970s a group of about a dozen Christians, Protestants and Catholics, began to meet in the Redemptorist monastery in Belfast, named Clonard. They gathered, usually once a fortnight, over a period of seven years; shared the Scriptures, discussed their various traditions and perceptions, and prayed together.

During this period in Northern Ireland the hunger strikes occurred. Ten young men from the Irish Republican Movement starved themselves to death in prison to obtain, from the Government, the right to be regarded as political prisoners. This was for the whole of Northern Ireland a very divisive issue, and the little Clonard group was not immune. But the members never left the meeting without sharing a sign of peace and an embrace.

After seven years members began to feel the call to a deeper sharing of life and witness. The immediate difficulty was where to find suitable premises. It was resolved in a way which can only be called providential.

The group located two old, semi-detached houses, situated in West Belfast on the Springfield Road. This was significant, since this road constitutes the 'Peace Line' in West Belfast, and forms the interface between the Protestant and Catholic communities. If the group was to be a witness to the reconciling love of Christ, what better place to exercise this ministry? The Sir Cyril Black Trust purchased the houses, and the first members, two Catholic sisters and a Methodist teacher, moved in just before Christmas 1982.

The name 'Cornerstone' is a clear reference to Jesus. For an ecumenical community, Ephesians 2:11-21 is especially significant, for there Paul speaks both of the Cornerstone, and of 'breaking down the dividing wall'.

The community is a *parable of possibility* on the Peace Line. It is involved in youth work, parents and toddlers groups and social work, including a senior citizens lunch club. It networks with many church groups and government agencies in the ongoing mission of bringing the peace of Christ to its troubled country.

Contact address: 443-445 Springfield Road, Belfast BT12 7DL.
Tel. 028 9032 1649.
e-mail: cornerstone@dnet.co.uk

Daily Bread Co-operative

In 1976 a Christian house group formed Daily Bread, wanting to take the Gospel of sharing and mutual support into the workplace. We are a co-operative owned and controlled by our Christian members, and started trading on 1 October 1980, with a working group of three. We have now grown to a staff of 20, with sales of over a million per annum.

We are both a viable business and an organisation with explicit social and spiritual objectives, expressing concern for our fellow workers, fellow human beings and the wider environment.

We trade as suppliers of wholefoods, carrying a large proportion of organic goods, dried fruits, nuts, seeds, herbs, spices, beans, grains, flakes, wholemeal and white flours, pastas, spreads, oils, drinks, fruit juices and mueslis, stocking in the region of 1,400 different products in varying sizes from 100g to 50kg. We do not stock anything that we know to be genetically modified.

We run a charity with our sister company Daily Bread Cambridge, through which donations to the Third World are made. Since 1984 a percentage of our gross wage bill has been donated, making a total of more than £100,000.

We offer employment in a supportive setting to people recovering from mental illness. They are paid on the same basis as members of the co-operative and expected to produce a good day's work in return. So we help them to adjust to the discipline of a working life, and prepare them for a return to open society.

Contact address: The Old Laundry, Bedford Road, Northampton NN4 7AD.
Tel. 01604 621531.
e-mail: northampton@dailybread.co.uk
website: www.dailybread.co.uk

The Darvell Bruderhof

In 1920 Eberhard Arnold, a well-known lecturer and writer, and his wife Emmy, left the comfort and security of his Berlin career and moved to Sannerz, a tiny German village, to found a small community based on the practices of the early Church.

Today this vision of Eberhard and Emmy Arnold is embodied in eight communities, each known as a Bruderhof, located in the UK, in the USA, and in Australia.

Christ's spirit and teachings in the Sermon on the Mount and throughout the Bible are both the goal and foundation of our communal life. We have no private property but share everything in common, as the early Christians did. Each member gives his or her talents, time and efforts wherever they are needed. Money and possessions are voluntarily pooled, and in turn each member is provided for and cared for. We meet daily for meals, fellowship, singing, prayer and decision-making. Though conscious of our weaknesses as individuals and as a group, we believe that Jesus' call can still be answered today.

We earn our living by the design, manufacture and sale of equipment for kindergartens and day-care centres, and also equipment for disabled persons, under the trade names of Community Playthings and Rifton Equipment. In addition, we publish books on radical discipleship and on the spiritual life, on social themes such as non-violence and justice, on children and the family, and on community life.

Contact address: The Darvell Bruderhof, Robertsbridge, East Sussex TN32 5DR. Tel. 01580 883300.
website: www.Plough.com

The Dominican Sisters of St Joseph

The sisters are an autonomous religious community of diocesan right (Diocese of Portsmouth). We were formally established on 5 July 1994 and were affiliated to the Order of Preachers by the Master General, Fr Timothy Radcliffe, on 8 March 1995. Being newly established, we have at present only one house in England, in the New Forest, Hampshire.

The sisters have been inspired by the action of St Dominic who, in the thirteenth century, drew women into a life of prayer and penance associated with the 'holy preaching' of the friars. It is this coming together of a fervent life in common, shaped by monastic observance, and a zeal for the work of preaching the Gospel for the salvation of souls, which characterises and defines our community. We are a contemplative–apostolic community.

In our age, which is more and more devoid of a sense of the sacred and indifferent to the life of the Church, our vocation is to be a strong contemplative presence in the midst of the world and to undertake those ministerial duties which are compatible with this primary goal of the community: to give praise to God and in him respond to the deepest longings of the hearts of our brothers and sisters in the world. We place special emphasis on the celebration of the liturgy, with daily mass, sung office, a life lived in common, the wearing of the Dominican habit, times of silence, personal and shared study, following to a large extent the ancient pattern of Dominican conventual life.

Our main apostolate is preaching and teaching the faith by: giving retreats in our retreat house; giving talks in parishes nearby and further afield; leading missions in parishes; catechesis of young children and those who wish to enter the Catholic Church; spiritual formation of schoolchildren and youth groups who attend the priory; welcoming ecumenical groups; facilitating a flourishing Dominican laity group which is attached to the priory; fostering vocations to the priesthood and religious life; working in collaboration with the Dominican Fathers in England, the USA and Portugal, who visit us.

Contact address: St Dominic's Priory, Shirley Holmes Road, Lymington, Hampshire SO41 8NH. Tel. 01590 681874.

The Ecumenical Society of the Blessed Virgin Mary

The Society was conceived in the autumn of 1966 at a reception given by Cardinal Suenens at his residence in Malines. This reception marked the fortieth anniversary of the last of the Malines Conversations, which brought together Anglican and Roman Catholic theologians seeking a road to unity between their two Churches.

Cardinal Mercier, who was Archbishop of Malines from 1906 to 1926, had been motivated to support these conversations by a consideration of the farewell discourse of Jesus, recorded in chapter 13 of John's gospel: 'I give you a new commandment: love one another; just as I have loved you, you also must love one another. By this love you have for one another, everyone will know that you are my disciples.'

Those who took part in that last meeting in 1926 left in a despondent mood, and would not have been able to foresee any reason for a celebration. Cardinal Suenens, however, provided one in his own person. He had been a seminarian in the Belgian College in Rome when the conversations took place, and was befriended by one of the participants. Suenens was involved in the preparatory work for the Second Vatican Council, and was one of its four moderators. He undoubtedly had some influence on the council's *Decree on Ecumenism*.

The Society which he helped to bring into being enables members of different Christian traditions to meet each other. It aims to dispel the misunderstanding, ignorance, and prejudice which keep Christians apart.

Contact address: 11 Belmont Road, Wallington, Surrey SM6 8TE.
Tel. 0208 647 5992.

The Emmanuel Community

The community is a Catholic Association of Christians from all states of life; it includes lay people both married and single, men and women consecrated in celibacy, and priests. In 1998 there were 6,000 committed members in nearly 50 countries, including England, Scotland and Ireland. A lay man, Pierre Goursat, founded the community in Paris in 1976, and in 1992 the Vatican officially recognised the community statutes.

Emmanuel means 'God with us', and he is with us in our daily life. We try to recognise Jesus as the centre of our lives in order to be 'in the world, without being of the world'. The profound grace of the community comes from eucharistic adoration. From this adoration is born compassion for all who are dying of hunger, both materially and spiritually. And from this compassion is born a thirst to evangelise throughout the whole world, reaching especially the poorest of the poor. Graces are drawn too from the sacraments, especially the Eucharist and reconciliation.

The community works with youth, with married and engaged couples and families (Love and Truth), with people in the working world (Presence and Witness), and with artists (Magnificat). Approximately 150,000 people participate every year in the activities of the community.

Every summer, the community organises a series of International Sessions on Christian Life in Paray-le-Monial, in France. One is dedicated to the family, another to the sick. The last session is an opportunity for young people to enter deeply into a living experience of their Catholic faith.

Community life is adapted to the normal daily round in the modern world, and to the personal circumstances in which members find themselves.

Contact address: 40 Grafton Road, Acton, London W3 68B.
Tel. 0208 993 9914.

The Focolare Movement

When Chiara Lubich started to meet with a group of friends in the air-raid shelters of Trent in Northern Italy during the Second World War, they had no idea that they were at the beginning of an incredible adventure that was to take them to the four corners of the earth. Their only desire was to love God and to live his word. One 'word' in particular struck them:' ... that they may all be one ... so that the world may believe' (John 17:21). They started to live mutual love in order always to have the presence of Jesus in their midst. This witness attracted people from all walks of life who gave the group a nickname, *focolare*, which means hearth or fireplace, because of the spiritual warmth which came from them.

After the war, this new spirituality began to spread, first to other towns and cities in Italy, then to the rest of Europe, and finally to all five continents. In Britain the movement had an ecumenical dimension right from the beginning, with members of various Christian traditions living the Focolare spirituality while remaining members of their own Churches. But the Focolare movement is not only ecumenical. There are ongoing dialogues with Muslims, Buddhists and members of other great faiths, as there are with people of good will who do not have a religious faith. The movement's official name is 'The Work of Mary'. Mary's task was to give Jesus to the world and it is that which remains the Focolare's prime objective.

Contact address: Focolare, 62 Kings Avenue, London SW4 8BM.
Tel. 020 8671 8355.

The Franciscan Friars of the Renewal

The community was begun in April 1987 by a group of Capuchin friars desiring to work more definitively for personal and communal renewal and the reform of the Church called for by the Holy Father and many spiritual leaders since Vatican II. By seeking a constant return to the sources of the whole Christian life and to the primitive inspiration of the Rule and Testament of St Francis, this community is attempting to live sincerely and truthfully a life in conformity to the Gospel and to the ideas of the Seraphic Father as handed on by the Capuchin tradition.

This community is seeking to live the vows of authentic Franciscan life in a way that effectively challenges the worldly values prevalent in every age. Material poverty, manual labour, complete renunciation of ownership of immovable property, mature and faithful chastity, an active and responsible obedience, and living with and engaging in hands-on work with the materially poor and destitute are essential components of this reform. The spiritual values uniting the friars are personal and communal commitment to Jesus Christ, our Saviour, through contemplative and liturgical prayer, daily eucharistic adoration, devotion to our Lady, imitation of St Francis and St Clare, love for the Church and loyalty to the Holy Father. To preserve the spirit and life of St

Francis in their apostolate, the friars carry on the work of evangelisation by preaching and other non-parochial ministry in the manner of the early Capuchin reform.

It is our hope that, despite our inconsistencies and weaknesses, we may present to our Christian sisters and brothers and to all others a prophetic witness of Christ's teaching that life is a pilgrimage of committed faith, trusting hope, and effective love of God and neighbour through the work of the Holy Spirit.

The friars opened their first house in England on 1 June 2000. They are located in Canning Town in the East End of London. Their ministry there includes a lunchtime drop-in centre, a night shelter, and recreational programmes for young people. They are also involved in Youth 2000 retreats, pro-life work and various kinds of preaching events.

Contact address: St Fidelis Friary, Killip Close, London E16 1LX.
Tel. 020 7474 0766.

The Community of St Fursey

The community, established in 1998, is a small group of Orthodox Christians, married or single, living in their own homes. The members join together in prayer two or three times a week. A mission, attached to the community house, produces mounted icon prints for sale, and supplies booklets on the faith of the Orthodox Church.

The community belongs to the British Antiochian Orthodox Deanery, which is part of the Patriarchate of Antioch.

The community's patron, St Fursey, was born in Ireland in about 600AD, and became a monk. As a pilgrim for Christ he left his monastery and homeland, and came to East Anglia in 633. King Sigebert gave him the remains of the Roman fort of Burgh Castle near Great Yarmouth, and in the safety of its massive walls he built a monastery. The Venerable Bede tells us that St Fursey 'was renowned for his words and works, and was outstanding in goodness'.

Contact address: St Fursey's House, 111 Neville Road, Sutton, Stalham, Norfolk NR12 9RR. Tel. 01692 580552.

The Hengrave Community

The Hengrave Community was an initiative of the Sisters of the Assumption. It was founded in 1974 as an ecumenical community to work for reconciliation between the Churches.

Today a mixed community of lay people, from many Christian traditions and many countries of the world, live alongside the sisters. They are mostly young, and have discovered at Hengrave an opportunity to grow, to explore relationships and their own faith, in an atmosphere of trust and celebration.

The community is based in a large Tudor house, which it runs as a conference centre. There is also a youth centre and – for those who want more of an adventure holiday – a barn. The community especially encourages groups which bring together those who are often apart – Christian and Jew, black and white, able and disabled. It also runs its own programme of quiet days and retreats.

The place itself works a change in those who come – the ancient walls steeped in history, the serene Suffolk landscape, the centuries of prayer and the daily cycle of praise. Hengrave is a place of reconciliation and healing, a place which brings together and mends.

Contact address: Hengrave Hall, Bury St Edmunds, Suffolk IP28 6LZ.
Tel. 01284 701561.

The Hope Community

The community was founded in 1985 by three members of a Roman Catholic order, Sisters of the Infant Jesus, who were invited by the local parish priest of St Patrick's in Wolverhampton to undertake a census of the Heath Town estate. Heath Town had a bad reputation. They found many people who felt isolation, loneliness and fear. In October of the same year the sisters became tenants, and they still live in maisonettes on the estate.

In line with our charism we work in partnership with laity where possible, seeking together ways:

- to form relationships with people with concern for those who are most isolated;
- to create opportunities for people to be involved in what we are about;
- to have the family as our focus;
- to find opportunities to develop gospel and family values;
- to provide the opportunity to share life and faith, and to celebrate this through group and community gatherings.

In 1999, in partnership with Father Hudson's Society (the social care agency for the Catholic Archdiocese of Birmingham), we opened the Hope Family Centre, which is run by a team of four project workers who share our charism. The aim of the centre is to provide a warm and welcoming environment where families feel free to come and seek help, to build relationships with others in similar situations, and to support each other. We aim to encourage parents to develop their self-worth. The centre works closely with the local Wolverhampton College and offers training and education with crèche facilities provided.

Contact address: 122 Clover Ley, Heath Town, Wolverhampton WV10 0HD. Tel. 01902 453590.

The House of the Open Door

The community was founded in 1978 by Roy and June Hendy. Its home is now in the Cotswolds, where it has a farm, a retreat centre and a pottery. Our daily time of worshipping God, and listening to him through each other, is a constant source of power and direction. The prayers and poems in this collection are inspired by words received during these times.

We run summer camps for young people, and do outreach in schools and prisons. In February 2000 we launched the Crossroads Project, a round-the-year formation programme for those who are between school and university, or at a time of decision. They are invited to the community for two weeks or more of reflection and teaching.

The vision of our community is:

- to build a community of love;
- to live a simple lifestyle, seeking God deeply in all that we do;
- to commit ourselves totally – our lives, ourselves, our time, our money – to work together for the common good of our brothers and sisters, and to do whatever work the Lord would have us do;
- to acknowledge that our prayer life, in private and in community, is the first way to serve God and each other and those around us;
- to share with each other our hopes and fears, our joys and sorrows;
- to open our hearts to one another, and yet to respect one another in humility, sensitivity and caring;
- to reach out to the needy round about;
- to practise the presence of Christ in the market places;
- to live according to the Word in all its fullness (Bible study second only to prayer);
- to respect the leadership of the community;
- to work for harmony and unity in the body, acknowledging that all denominations are part of Christ's body on earth;
- to build an apostolate and discipleship group, rather than just making converts;
- by our prayer and our love to bring Christ's healing to each other and to those to whom the Lord may send us.

Contact address: Childswickham House, Childswickham, nr Broadway, Worcestershire WR12 7HH. Tel. 01386 852084.

The Iona Community

The community was founded in 1938 by the Revd George MacLeod, then a parish minister in Glasgow. It is an ecumenical Christian community that is committed to seeking new ways of living the Gospel in today's world. Initially this purpose was expressed through the rebuilding of the monastic quarters of the medieval abbey on Iona and pursued in mission and ministry through-out Scotland and beyond. The community today remains committed to rebuilding the common life through working for social and political change, striving for the renewal of the Church with an ecumenical emphasis, and exploring new, more inclusive approaches to worship.

The community now has over 240 members, about 1,500 associate members and around 1,500 friends. The members comprise women and men (lay and ordained) from many backgrounds and denominations, living throughout Britain, with a few overseas. They are committed to a five-fold rule involving a daily devotional discipline, sharing, and accounting for their use of time and money, regular meeting, and action for justice and peace.

The community is not an alternative Church, and has formal links with the Church of Scotland and the ecumenical bodies in Britain. Members are involved in local congregations, and in their own situations express the com-mitment of the community to a number of concerns: the promotion of peace and justice, through, for example, opposing nuclear weapons and seeking a reduction in the arms trade; supporting the cause of the poor and exploited in Britain and abroad; political activity in combating racism; engagement with environmental and constitutional issues; the exploration of human sexuality; commitment to strengthening interdenominational understanding and the sharing of communion; concern for young people; the promotion of inter-faith dialogue; the rediscovery of an approach to spirituality appropriate to our times, and the development of the ministry of healing.

The community has three residential centres: the Abbey and the MacLeod Centre on Iona, and Camas Adventure Camp on the Ross of Mull. Its adminis-trative headquarters are in Glasgow, which also serves as a base for work with young people, for the Wild Goose Resource Group, who work in the field of worship, for a bimonthly magazine, *Coracle*, and for a publishing house, Wild Goose Publications.

Contact address: Pearce Institute, 840 Govan Road, Glasgow G51 3UU.
Tel. 0141 445 4561.
e-mail:ionacomm@gla.iona.org.uk

For enquiries about visiting Iona, please contact Iona Abbey, Isle of Iona, Argyll PA76 6SN. Tel. 01681 700404.
e-mail: ionacomm@iona.org.uk

L'Arche

The first British community of L'Arche was opened in 1977, 14 years after Jean Vanier founded L'Arche with Raphael Simi and Philippe Seux in France. There are now eight communities in Britain and 120 around the world. Community life is focused on our houses, where people with and without learning disabilities choose to live together. Most communities also run day projects and workshops where the opportunity to do creative and worthwhile work is offered.

L'Arche communities in Britain are Christian and ecumenical, and include members who belong to most of the main British denominations and traditions. Living in ecumenical communities requires us to be creative with our liturgies and prayer life, and to work at understanding each other's traditions. We welcome people regardless of religious affiliation, but we ask all who come to respect our Christian roots and our commitment to our local parishes.

Our lifestyle is rooted in the needs and gifts of every day, because it is through the ordinariness of daily life that we rediscover the depth of the Gospel and the love of God for each one of us. In seeking to listen to the voices and choices of people with learning disabilities we have learnt that God's kingdom is one of upside-down values: where the rejected take their place at the centre; where those cared for are found to have the most to give; where the voiceless become eloquent.

Contact address: 10 Briggate, Silsden, Keighley, West Yorkshire BD20 9JT. Tel. 01535 656186.

The Madonna House Community

When God wishes to accomplish a great work, he speaks to someone. Thus, the multitude of communities in the Church, down through the centuries, were first born in the hearts of individuals. These gifted people lived the Gospel in such a dynamic and attractive way that others were drawn to live according to their charism.

The foundress of the Madonna House Community was the servant of God Catherine de Hueck Doherty (whose cause for sainthood is now under way). She was a Russian refugee who, after personal experience of the Russian revolution, the First World War, the Depression in North America, and her own personal struggles, decided that only by people living the Gospel radically could the world be renewed and restored.

In the early 1930s she literally sold all she possessed and started working with the poor in Toronto; then with the Black people in Harlem, New York. Returning to Canada in 1947, she entered the depths of the charism she was given by applying the Gospel to every aspect of life within a community of men and women, priests and laity, who were attracted by her profound and living faith in Christ.

Whether at the main centre of the community, in Combermere, Ontario, or in the smaller houses, she taught that the love of the members, one for the other, was the greatest witness that could be given. The apostolate of the Madonna House Community encompasses many dimensions – soup kitchens, retreats, counselling, publishing, or any other works the Spirit may call it to. But the heart of its charism is to evangelise the world by the example of the love of its members, one for another.

Contact address: Madonna House, Thorpe Lane, Robin Hood's Bay, North Yorkshire YO22 4TQ. Tel. 01947 880169.

The Maranatha Community

The community comprises thousands of committed Christians, scattered throughout the United Kingdom and abroad. They are active in all the main Churches, and include Anglicans, Roman Catholics, Methodists, Presbyterians, Baptists, Pentecostalists, Salvationists and members of the United Reformed, Independent and Orthodox Churches.

Maranatha is founded on three words – unity, renewal and healing. Members of the community are deeply aware that Christ calls us to be one, and therefore pray and work for Christian unity in a divided world. Maranatha recognises the call of Christ to new life, and therefore prays and works for renewal of faith, in a dying world. Maranatha is profoundly aware of Christ's call to wholeness, and prays and works for the extension of the Christian healing ministry in a sick world.

All this has led members into a deep concern for the poor and marginalised at home and abroad, with work among children and with the needs of the persecuted Church. Its healing ministry embraces collaboration with medical practitioners and also deep involvement for peace and reconciliation in Northern Ireland. Through its campaigning arm, it is an effective Christian voice for truth, justice and righteousness in the life of the nation.

Mother Teresa said to Maranatha at its foundation 20 years ago: 'If you pray without serving, your prayers will be in vain. If you serve without praying, your serving will be in vain.'

In Maranatha there is a balance between devotions and action, between listening together and proclaiming with one voice. There is also a balance between the new and the old, between liturgy and freedom in worship.

The community claims nothing for itself other than being little brothers and sisters of Jesus on pilgrimage together. Maranatha travels light. It possesses little, and its members endeavour to live and speak the simple Gospel. There is an urgency to its message today. It is not a Church. It is not a breakaway movement. It exists to serve the Kingdom and to support and hopefully enrich the Churches.

Contact address: 102 Irlam Road, Flixton, Manchester M41 6JT.
Tel. 0161 748 4858.

The Missionaries of Charity

The Society of the Missionaries of Charity was started by Mother Mary Teresa Bojaxhiu in India in 1950. The aim of the congregation is to quench the infinite thirst of Jesus Christ on the cross for love of souls by the profession of the evangelical counsels and wholehearted and free service to the poorest of the poor. The sisters strive through their ministry with the poor, sick and abandoned to make the mercy and love of God very real so as to help them turn to God with filial confidence.

In England we are in London, Birmingham, Liverpool and Newcastle; in Wales in Dowleis; in Scotland in Edinburgh and Glasgow, and in Ireland in Armagh. The sisters visit the housebound or the sick and render to them the humblest services. Sometimes we clean the house; at other times it is necessary just to sit and listen. We visit prisons and hospitals as well. In our visits to families, we encourage them to pray together and to receive the sacraments. We run temporary night shelters for men or women, which are dry houses. We also go out into the streets at night with hot soup, tea and sandwiches for the homeless. Our soup kitchens are places where the poor come together for a prayer and a hot meal. The sisters also work with children, preparing them for the sacraments or simply teaching them the Catholic faith. During the summer we run a scheme for those children who are not able to go away for the holidays.

We look on our work not as an end but as a means whereby we can put our love for Christ into action in every person we touch. As Christ said, 'When you did it to one of the least of these my brothers and sisters, you did it to me.'

Contact address: 177 Bravington Road, London W9 3AR. Tel. 0208 960 2644.

The Neocatechumenal Way

In 1964 a young painter named Kiko Argüello felt a call to share the life of the poor. He was drawn to Palomeras Altas, a shanty-town on the outskirts of Madrid, home to gypsies, prostitutes, tramps, robbers and poor immigrants. Taking a Bible and a guitar, he went to live among them, finding shelter in a shack with seven stray dogs.

Gradually his poor neighbours began to come and ask why he had joined them, and he would share with them his faith. Three years later the Archbishop of Madrid asked him to begin working in parishes, and so the neocatechumenal way was formed.'Born in the shanty-towns of Madrid like the tiny mustard seed of the Gospel,' said Pope John Paul II in 1997, 'in thirty years it has become a great tree which has now spread to more than one hundred countries.'

'For many,' said the Pope, 'the neocatechumenal experience has been a way of conversion and of maturation in the faith, through the rediscovery of Baptism as a true source of life, and of the Eucharist as the culminating moment of the existence of a Christian; through the rediscovery of the Word of God which, broken in fraternal communion, becomes the light and guide of life; and through the rediscovery of the Church as an authentic missionary community.'

Contact address: Church of St Charles Borromeo, 8 Ogle Street, London W1P 7LG. Tel. 020 7636 2883.

The Northumbria Community

The community consists of companions on a journey of pilgrimage and exploration. The pilgrimage is in response to the question. 'Who is it that you seek?' and the exploration in response to the question: 'How then shall we live?' The call on the community's life is to 'rebuild the ancient ruins and raise up the age-old foundations' of the Christian faith – inspiration and insights that have been largely lost but which can shed much light on our despairing world. Drawing in particular from the desert fathers and the era of the Celtic saints, the community echoes the words of Dietrich Bonhoeffer, who wrote: 'The renewal of the Church will come from a new type of monasticism which has in common with the old an uncompromising allegiance to the Sermon on the Mount. It is high time people banded together to do this.'

The community is geographically dispersed, but with a base at Hetton Hall in north Northumberland, not far from Holy Island. There are two key strands to its life: one emphasises the contemplative (seeking God in the cell of one's own heart); the other emphasises the apostolic (the need to take the monastery through mission into the market place). The community's growth and development have been enriched by diversity but underpinned by a common commitment to the Rule of Availability and Vulnerability – which is a call to risky living. The availability is both to God and to others (through hospitality, intercession and mission); the vulnerability is expressed through being teachable in the discipline of prayer, saturation in the Scriptures and being accountable to one another, often through soul friendships. It also means embracing the heretical imperative (challenging assumed truth), being receptive to constructive criticism, affirming that relationships matter more than reputation, and living openly among people as a church without walls.

These concepts and ideals are deliberately provocative, rather then prescriptive, and the experience of the individuals that comprise the community is that of constant failure to live up to them. Each has to work it out alone; but by being honest and real with each other, encouragement and strength is derived from being together.

Contact address: Hetton Hall, Chatton, Alnwick, Northumberland NE66 5SD. Tel. 01289 388235.
e-mail: northumbriacommunity@bigfoot.com
website: www.northumbriacommunity.org

The Pilgrims Community

The community was founded in 1989 by Sister Angela Murphy PBVM and Father Jonathan Cotton, a priest of the Catholic Diocese of Nottingham. Its purpose was to provide a year out for young people who wanted to be volunteer workers for the Church in the diocese. They initially assisted in sponsoring parishes, but are now trained within a supportive, long-term core community.

The community is centred on Christ and exists to promote the 'new evangelisation' called for by Pope John Paul II. We have a structured communal and prayer life, and offer a formation programme in discipleship and evangelisation. We also serve the local church and community through youth mission teams, prayer ministry and parish retreats. We have a school for evangelisation with a variety of courses, and do mission work in the Diocese of Livingstone, Zambia. We also offer a comprehensive training programme for adult parish evangelists.

Both married and single people commit themselves to the community for varying lengths of time, sometimes for life. They either work as full-time evangelists, or continue in secular work to support the community. Some are committed to consecrated life in the community, and others are exploring the possibility of being trained as priests for the Pilgrims.

Charitable status separate from the diocesan charity is being sought, and constitutions as a new community in line with canon law are currently being written. Under the guidance of the Holy Spirit, and with the support of the diocesan authorities and the leadership team of the Presentation Sisters, much prayer and discernment continues about the development of the community.

Contact address: Presentation Convent, Chesterfield Road, Matlock, Derbyshire DE4 3FS. Tel. 01629 57704.

The Community of the Prince of Peace

This Baptist religious community was founded in April 1997 in Carterton, Oxfordshire. The founder members felt called by God to explore the interface between the Baptist, evangelical and non-conformist traditions on the one hand, and the religious life on the other. The journey towards the establishment of the community included oversight by the Anglican priory at Burford. In May 1999 the community moved to Riddings, Derbyshire, to give space for more members and guests.

The community is listed as a Baptist organisation in the Baptist Union Directory and its official Visitor is the Revd Keith Jones, Rector of the International Baptist Theological Seminary in Prague. It is a member of the ecumenical Conference of Religious.

The community seeks to provide a resource for the Church. Prayer is a primary focus, and a four-fold rhythm of daily offices forms the essential structure of its prayer life. In addition, prayer is regularly offered for people in need, the Church at large and the world. The community welcomes individuals and small groups who seek quiet space for reflection, rest and retreat. It is a place simply to be, or to find a listening ear or more formal spiritual direction.

The community's home is an attractive Victorian house in two acres of grounds. It is set in a quiet area with views over parkland in which visitors to the community are free to walk. Guests of any denomination, or none, are very welcome and all can share in community prayers if they wish.

Contact address: Baptist monastery, 4 Church Street, Riddings, Alfreton, Derbyshire DE55 4BW. Tel. 01773 603533.
e-mail: commpp@ukonline.co.uk

The Community for Reconciliation

The community was begun as a network by John and Joan Johansen-Berg during their ministry in West London. In 1986 they moved to Worcestershire to form a small residential community which is a resource group for the action of a wider community, and which makes available a conference, retreat and training centre.

The community helps with renewal programmes, ecumenical missions and festivals of faith. It is also active in justice and peace, both in the United Kingdom and overseas. In particular, it has developed conflict-resolution and peace-building projects in Romania, East Africa (including Rwanda and Burundi) and Croatia, and has links in Italy, Ireland, Hungary and Israel-Palestine.

The focus of its work is reconciliation. Relationships are broken in many situations – between individuals and within families, in churches and between Churches, and in society at local, national and international levels. Reconciliation is positive and often costly. It involves finding a creative way forward where there are differences, healing where there is hurt, opposing injustice and oppression and working for peace.

The community seeks reconciliation within people, between people, and between God and people. This is brought about pre-eminently by Jesus Christ in his costly sacrifice, which restores the right relationship between God and his people.

Undergirding our work as a community is a life of prayer. The residential community gathers for shared prayer most mornings; we follow a pattern set down in several books, so that the wider network is able to share in this prayer life. While we are a committed Christian community, we seek to be in dialogue with people of other faiths and to share in action for justice and peace with all people of good will.

Contact address: Barnes Close, Chadwich, Bromsgrove, Worcestershire B61 0RA. Tel. 01562 710231.

The Sisters of the Gospel of Life

At the beginning of the Jubilee Year 2000, three young women, inspired by the Gospel of Life and with the support of Cardinal Winning, founded a religious community to promote the dignity of human life and to witness to Christ as Lord of all creation.

The community's primary mission is to centre its life on Jesus Christ through a call to personal holiness. To this end, the day is structured around personal and community prayer, the mass and adoration. Through contemplation, each member of the community seeks to deepen her relationship with Christ and then bring the fruits of that contemplation to others.

The community will continue the work of Cardinal Winning's Pro-Life Initiative, set up in 1997. This work consists of crisis pregnancy care, providing for the practical, emotional and spiritual needs of the women and families in need. The apostolate also addresses the promotion of the family, specifically Natural Family Planning and the Christian vision of sex and marriage.

The community is based on Pope John Paul II's encyclical *Evangelium Vitae*, which asserts: 'The Gospel of Life is at the heart of Jesus' message. Lovingly received day after day by the Church, it is to be preached with dauntless fidelity as the "Good News" to the people of every age and culture.'

The community conveys this Gospel by talking to parish and school groups; giving retreats to various groups including mothers, women who have had abortions and pro-life workers; organising times of prayer and meditation dedicated to recognising Christ, the Source of all life.

Contact address: Our Lady and St Joseph's, 106 Dixon Avenue, Glasgow G42 8EL. Tel. 0141 422 2634.
e-mail: GospelofLife@btinternet.com

The Sion Community for Evangelism

The community is a group of Catholic lay people, priests and religious who have joined together in a committed fellowship. We seek to proclaim the Gospel in a dynamic way, so that all who receive the Good News may themselves become active disciples. The community is active in helping to renew the life of the Church at grass roots and in equipping people for the task of evangelisation. We try to bring together traditional Catholic spirituality and the fresh outpouring of the Holy Spirit which many people experience today. The Sion Community always works under the authority of the bishops in whose dioceses we operate.

Our evangelisation ministry comprises mission teams working in the UK and Ireland. We have parish teams, a primary school team, and our youth ministry 'Cross Purposes'. To complement our itinerant mission work we also have SENT, our national training centre in Brentwood, Essex. Here we run a variety of courses in evangelisation and leadership throughout the year.

Contact address: SENT, Sawyers Hall Lane, Brentwood, Essex CM15 9BX.
Tel. 01277 215011.
website: www.sioncommunity.org

The Solace Community

The community is the home of 'Mothers' Prayers', a network of prayer groups for mothers who wish to pray together for their children and grandchildren, and for all spiritual mothers.

Veronica Williams writes:

Over a period of time, my sister-in-law Sandra and I had felt a growing need to pray in a more committed way, in order to combat the problems facing our children. On two occasions Sandra had been awakened in the night with the words: 'Pray for your children.'

During this period – when I prayed that the Lord would keep us on the right path – I opened the Bible at Jeremiah 31:16:

> Stop your crying and wipe away your tears.
> All that you have done for your children will not go unrewarded.
> They will return from the enemy's land.

We felt that the Lord placed on our hearts, right at the beginning, that he was the boss and that we were his secretaries.

The prayer group, which started in November 1995, has spread to many countries throughout the world. This is in spite of the fact that we have not initiated any publicity and we have only given talks about Mothers' Prayers when invited.

Such blessings have come though Mothers' Prayers, with many children coming back to their Faith, coming home after long absences, and finding work and accommodation. It is such a blessing for mothers too, to be able to share their pain in a Christian, confidential way; and through the weekly meetings a great love and compassion have developed.

The Solace Community itself has drawn together a number of local Christians, who say the community prayer each day and help with the administration of the Mothers' Prayers office. They also do cleaning, cooking and gardening and make sure that everything runs smoothly.

Contact address: PO Box 822, Gravesend, Kent DA13 9ZZ. Tel. 01474 834084.

Verbum Dei

Verbum Dei is an international Catholic community, which was founded by Fr Jaime Bonet in Mallorca, Spain, in 1963. It received pontifical approval in the year 2000 as an Institution of Consecrated Life in the Catholic Church.

The community is an international family united by one and the same charism and mission. There are three branches: celibate women, priests who consecrate their lives to God with the profession of vows, and missionary couples who consecrate themselves to God through the sacrament of marriage. The community extends to and embraces people of all states and ages: single and married, old and young, students, people of different backgrounds and occupations.

We seek to be a clear expression of the Kingdom of God, building up Christian communities of living faith through prayer, witness of life and the ministry of the Word.

Prayer is an integral and vital part of the community's daily life. It is in intimate dialogue with the Word, or prayer, that our calling and mission to preach the Gospel is rooted. Preaching the Word of God is for us transmitting the life of God that we receive in prayer. An essential part of our mission is enabling others to do the same. We aim always to precede and accompany our preaching by a witness of life that makes it credible.

Contact address: Verbum Dei Centre, Nunnery Lane, Carisbrooke, Isle of Wight PO30 1YR. Tel. 01983 529554.

Youth 2000

Youth 2000 is an international spiritual initiative run by young people for young people. It seeks to encourage and affirm them, and to build them up in the Catholic faith. Working in co-operation with older people and religious, the charity provides a programme of youth festivals and other spiritual events throughout Europe and other parts of the world.

The words of Pope John Paul II in 1989, on the occasion of the World Youth Day at Santiago de Compostella, provided the inspiration for this work. His Holiness there called for young people to be 'witnesses of the love of God and of faith'. In response to this invitation a young Englishman called Ernest Williams founded Youth 2000.

Since that time the initiative has spread like wildfire, and now has active groups in several continents. The focus of the work is the organisation of Eucharist-centred retreats, and prayer festivals during which the Blessed Sacrament is perpetually exposed. At the festivals young people hear talks about church teaching, receive the sacraments and are introduced to Mary, the Mother of God, in the life of the Church. The charity also promotes the setting up of Eucharist-centred youth groups and encourages young people to become involved in pro-life work.

Youth 2000 has already seen thousands of young people find their spiritual home in the Catholic Church. In the words of one young person who came to an event, 'I can honestly say that I felt God. God extended his hand and we took hold.'

Contact address: PO Box 176, Leeds LS17 9XU. Tel. 01937 579700.

Sources and acknowledgements

The idea for this book came from Brendan Walsh of Darton, Longman and Todd, who steered it through with characteristic good humour.

I am grateful to a number of people for helping me to identify communities to contact, especially Kristina Cooper from the Catholic Charismatic Renewal Centre, Stratford Caldecott from Plater College, Archbishop Rowan Williams, Anthony Kramers from L'Arche Edinburgh, and my brother Petroc, from the Maryvale Institute.

Thanks also to: Carl and Marylee Mitcham, who gave me my first experience of Christian community in the Knob Country of Kentucky; Brian and Rosemary O'Malley, who went all out for God, and who laid the foundations of my faith in the mountains of South Wales; the Sisters of the Assumption, who gave me one of the happiest years of my life in the Hengrave Community; all at L'Arche who have celebrated with me, and have encouraged me to stay faithful to the Gospel.

Thanks to my daughter Nadia, for helping with the typing.

And thanks to our Saviour Jesus Christ, for giving me such an interesting and wonderful life – which made this book possible.

Thanks to the individuals and communities who have contributed the prayers below.

The Community of Aidan and Hilda and The Bowthorpe Ecumenical Community
The prayers are by Ray Simpson. Most are reproduced, with his permission, from his book *Celtic Worship throughout the Year* (Hodder and Stoughton, 1997).

Clare Priory
'Make your home in me' is based on the spirituality of St Augustine of Hippo, and was written by Ben O'Rourke OSA, Michael Teader and Zoe Collings. The 'Prayer to the Mother of Good Counsel' is by Pauline Edwards.

The Columbanus Community
'The primal garden' is by the Revd Glenn Barclay.

Darvell Bruderhof
The prayers are by Heini Arnold, from his book *May Thy Light Shine* (Plough Publishing, 1986).

The Dominican Sisters of St Joseph
The 'Prayer to the Holy Spirit' and 'A heart set free' are by St Thomas Aquinas.

The Ecumenical Society of the Blessed Virgin Mary
These prayers come from *An Ecumenical Office of Mary, the Mother of Jesus,* which is available from the Society. Thanks to Stratford Caldecott for pointing out this publication to me. The 'Anthem to the Virgin Mary' comes from Mount St Bernard Abbey; 'The overshadowing' is by Cheslyn Jones.

The Emmanuel Community
'Mary, servant of the Lord' is adapted from a prayer by St Louis Grignion de Montfort, and appears in *Éditions de l'Emmanuel* (1998).

Focolare
The prayers are by its founder, Chiara Lubich.

The Franciscan Friars of the Renewal
The 'Prayer to St Francis' is by Pope John Paul II.

The Hengrave Community
'Bring together' is by Mgr Ronald Knox; 'Child of hope' by Judith Carter; 'The light of Christ' by Anthea Dove; 'Bless the Lord' by Sister Julian. 'The dove of peace' was contributed by the Bishop of St Edmundsbury's Course, and 'The diamond' by RAF Bentwaters. The Exultet and the Reproaches are traditional Christian prayers; 'Holy Thursday Supper' a traditional Jewish prayer.

The Iona Community
'The Master Carpenter', 'Signs of dawn' and 'A prayer for Iona' are from the *Iona Community Worship Book* (1992). 'The exiles in our midst' is by Kathy Galloway; 'We are here' by Ruth Burgess; 'Star kindler' and 'Cross-carrying Jesus' by the Revd Kate McIlhagga; 'Prepare us for your way' by Alison Adam; 'The brightness of truth' by Douglas Galbraith; 'A prayer for Hiroshima Day' by Helen Steven; these pieces come from *The Pattern of our Days* (1996). 'Goodness is stronger' and 'For the hungry' are from *A Wee Worship Book* (1999), 'Open our eyes' from *Cloth for the Cradle* (1997), and 'Ride on in majesty' from *Stages on the Way* (1998); these are all by the Wild Goose Worship Group. We are grateful to Wild Goose Publications for permission to reproduce all the above copyright material here.

'Beyond our boundaries' is by Jan Sutch Pickard and appeared in *Vice Versa* (Church in the Market Place Publications). 'A place of hope' is by Peter Millar, and previously appeared in *An Iona Prayer Book* (Canterbury Press, 1998).

L'Arche Edinburgh
The prayers come from da Noust, the members and friends of L'Arche Edinburgh responsible for creative activities. Da Noust is Oracadian for a boat shelter, a place to withdraw for rest and renewal before the working day ahead. 'Chew on the gospel' is based on the spirituality of friends and members of the Hermitage of the Transfiguration at Roslin in Scotland.

L'Arche Lambeth
'The washing of the feet' was written by an ecumenical group commissioned by the International Council of L'Arche. The final version incorporates suggestions from the World Council of Churches and the Lambeth Conference of 1998.

'A door of hope' is by Jean Vanier, and was previously published in a book of the same name (Hodder and Stoughton, 1996). 'The miserable child', 'Do I dare' and 'Two prisons' are also by Jean, and come from his book *Tears of Silence* (Darton, Longman and Todd, 1991). 'Unlock our hearts' is by Thérèse Vanier, and previously appeared in *One Bread, One Body* (Novalis/Gracewing, 1997). Thanks to Jean and Thérèse for permission to reproduce these prayers here.

The Madonna House Community
The prayers are by its founder, Catherine de Hueck Doherty. All come from her book *Jesus: Prayers from the Diaries of Catherine de Hueck Doherty* (Madonna House Publications, Combermere, Ontario, 1996), except for the prayer for priests, which comes from her unpublished diaries.

The Maranatha Community
The prayers are by the community's leader, Dennis Wrigley.

The Missionaries of Charity
The meditations are by Mother Teresa of Calcutta. They are reproduced here by kind permission of Sister Nirmala, Superior General of the Missionaries of Charity.

The Northumbria Community
'Walking with grief' is by Andy Raine. 'Prayer of the heart' comes from the Cuthbert liturgy, and the blessings at the doorway and in the kitchen from the Brigid liturgy. In midday prayer, the words of 'Teach us, dear Lord' come from Psalm 90, as arranged by Jim Patterson in *The Singing Word*, published by Youth with a Mission. The final blessing is by St Teresa of Avila ('Teresa's bookmark'). The 'Blessing on those departing' comes from Morning Prayer, and was originally written as 'Peter's song for Marygate' by Peter Sutcliffe.

All the pieces are reproduced with permission from *Celtic Daily Prayer*, © 2000 The Northumbria Community Trust Ltd (HarperCollins, 2000).

The Pilgrims Community
'A prayer to Mary' is by Fr Jonathan Cotton; 'Night blessing' is by Alex Heath; 'Come, Holy Spirit' is by Alex Heath and Fr Jonathan; 'Jericho' and 'Is there anything I can do' are by Joanna Jensen. These last four pieces appear as songs on the cassette and CD *Let the people know*, which is available from the Pilgrims Community.

The Community for Reconciliation
The prayers are by John Johansen-Berg, and previously appeared in *Prayers of Prophecy*, published by the community in 1990.

The Sisters of the Gospel of Life
'The Gospel of Life' comes at the end of *Evangelium Vitae*, an encyclical by Pope John Paul II.

The Solace Community
'Mothers Prayers' and 'One family' are extracted from the booklet *Mothers' Prayers*, which is available from the community.

Youth 2000
'Radiating Christ' is adapted from a prayer by John Henry Newman.